HOPE
FOR AMERICA'S YOUTH

BEYOND THE BLUE DOORS
OF A BOYS & GIRLS CLUB

JANE EDWARDS SUTTER

◆ FriesenPress

One Printers Way
Altona, MB R0G 0B0
Canada

www.friesenpress.com

Copyright © 2024 by Jane Edwards Sutter
First Edition — 2024

All rights reserved.

No part of this publication may be reproduced in any form, or by any means, electronic or mechanical, including photocopying, recording, or any information browsing, storage, or retrieval system, without permission in writing from FriesenPress.

ISBN
978-1-03-830525-1 (Hardcover)
978-1-03-830524-4 (Paperback)
978-1-03-830526-8 (eBook)

1. PSYCHOLOGY, INTERPERSONAL RELATIONS

Distributed to the trade by The Ingram Book Company

Table of Contents

IN PRAISE OF vi

INTRODUCTION ix

CHAPTER 1 1
From Suicide to Strength
    Jessica 1

CHAPTER 2 13
Just Three Caring Women

CHAPTER 3 21
The Universal Language of Hope
    Sergio 21

CHAPTER 4 31
Rejection Opens the Door to Vision and Purpose

CHAPTER 5 39
Pathways to Self-Acceptance
    AnaMarie 39
    Leo 44

CHAPTER 6 49
For Such a Time as This

CHAPTER 7 61
Rising Resilience
    Veronica 61

CHAPTER 8 67
Purpose Bigger than a Paycheck
    LaRissa Conn 67
    A. Jaye Johnson 72
    Sharon Gordon Linton 75

CHAPTER 9 77
Better than a Bon Jovi Concert
    Adan 77

CHAPTER 10 83
The Family Business
    Rick Nagel 84
    Jennifer Fogg Lickteig 88
    Carl Anderson 89

CHAPTER 11 93
When All Else Fails, Love Remains
    Mary Kate 93

CHAPTER 12 103
Volunteer Keys
    Donna Leftwich 103
    Wes Haddox 106
    Suzanne Breedlove 108

CHAPTER 13 111
Bridging Boundaries

CHAPTER 14 123
Many Ways to Mentor

PERSONAL EPILOGUE 135

REFERENCES 145

ACKNOWLEDGMENTS 149

ABOUT THE AUTHOR 151

IN PRAISE OF

Hope for America's Youth is an inspirational must read for anyone working or volunteering with our communities' most vulnerable youth. The author gives direct examples of how caring adults in the lives of our kids can change the future in a positive and impactful manner. It is truly life changing!
  —Debby Hampton, former CEO of the United Way of
  Central Oklahoma

Hope for America's Youth: Beyond the Blue Doors of a Boys and Girls Club provides just what the title promises. Each story Jane Sutter shares about what club members carried on their shoulders as they walked through the blue doors is deeply personal. None of these profiles are about kids whose home lives were easy, and all found hope and tools for life through membership at the Boys & Girls Club. Readers will be heartbroken by the pain and truly inspired by the strength and resiliency of these kids who have overcome so much. This book is a primer on what can happen when nonprofits work well, and a hard look at the many societal issues that still need to be addressed to keep our children safe.
  —Mary Mélon-Tully, President/CEO Oklahoma City Public
  Schools Foundation

Hope for America's Youth is the heartwarming and inspirational story of Jane Sutter's transformation from a government official to running the Boys & Girls Clubs of Oklahoma County. Along the way, the word "transformation" took on a whole new meaning. Jane saw disadvantaged and at-risk children overcome issues of self-image, abusive caregivers, and being born into a hostile world and be "transformed" by staff and positive adult role models into successful adults.

You will read about boys and girls who had little hope when they walked through the Clubs doors. The time-tested principles and values of the Club literally saved their lives and gave them educational and social opportunities to escape from the clutches of poverty or lack of developmental support. Jane's passion to chronicle the events of the life-changing events of children comes through loud and clear.

I promise you. If you read Jane's story of hundreds of frightened and underserved children, you will become an advocate of her theory that helping children reach their potential should be society's number one priority.

—Bob Burke, Constitutional Lawyer and Author

Jane's *Hope for America's Youth* perfectly illustrates the Spirit of the Boys & Girls Club Movement from the perspectives of those who serve and are served. It is clear that this work is a calling, and I am grateful she answered.

—Robin Schmidt, Former Director of Organizational Development, BGCA - SW

Jane Sutter's path of servant leadership warrants study by anyone searching for personal meaning and in pursuit of societal impact, which should include all of us! What a story she has to tell!

—Clifford Hudson, Former CEO, Sonic Corp.

Hope for America's Youth, Beyond the Blue Doors of a Boys & Girls Club is a compelling exploration of the author's experiences working with young individuals. Through poignant storytelling, Sutter delves into the lives of youth who have triumphed against all odds, as well as those who have faced challenges beyond their control. The book shines a spotlight on the crucial role that positive role models and evidence-based programming play in shaping the lives of young people.

Sutter's writing is both insightful and inspiring, offering a glimpse into the world of youth development and the profound impact that support systems can have on the trajectory of a young person's life. Through heartfelt narratives and thought-provoking reflections, *Hope for America's Youth* serves as a powerful reminder of the resilience and potential inherent in each individual.

This book is a must-read for anyone passionate about youth empowerment and the transformative power of mentorship and structured programming. Sutter's words resonate long after the final page, leaving readers with a renewed sense of hope and determination for the future of America's youth.

—Zana Williams, Founder and CEO of Mindful Resolutions

INTRODUCTION

There are many paths that might lead a person to write a book. Mine began in 2020, at the age of sixty-seven, when I retired from the Boys & Girls Clubs of Oklahoma County. With new freedom and time in retirement, which happened to coincide with the start of a global pandemic, I began to reflect on my nearly ten years as the president and chief executive officer (CEO) of that nationally acclaimed after-school program for underserved and at-risk children and teens. I thought about the hundreds of young people I had seen creating better futures for themselves as they worked with helpful adult role models. I reflected on the talented staff members and generous volunteers who had helped guide so many of these talented young people out of poverty onto paths toward higher education and self-sufficiency.

I had complete confidence that Teena Belcik, the person who followed me as president and CEO, would do an incredible job leading the organization. Yet I had a nagging feeling that I had unfinished business. Had I in some way abandoned the kids I'd known through the Boys & Girls Club? Many of them had been let down by so many adults in their lives; did I owe them something more beyond my tenure leading the organization?

Did our time together instill hope for the future, and if so, how? Their stories, and my time as president of the Club, helped shape the person I am. Was that true in reverse? Was our after-school program really a transformative part of their lives? Did we positively usher them into adulthood and perhaps parenthood, or did we adults have inflated assumptions about the part we played? And, thinking even more wholistically, what would the impact be, if any, on future generations?

When I was a teenager, I read a book called *Magnificent Obsession* by Lloyd Douglas, the popular American author and minister. That book, published in 1929, subsequently was made into two motion pictures of the same name—one starring Rock Hudson—and remained popular for years. My takeaway, which has stayed with me for several decades now, is that each interaction a person has with another human being changes both people in some way. The change may be miniscule, but it's real. And sometimes the change is dramatic.

While I had watched kids at the Boys & Girls Clubs find their passions and purpose through various programs, sports, academic help, recognition, and community engagement, I came to believe that the real magic in their transformations grew from the positive multi-year relationships they were able to establish with their mentors at the Club. And I believe that their mentors were changed by those relationships as well. I know I was.

I've seen countless examples of compassionate adults helping young people take control of their lives and forge a better future. Their stories appear to me like a scattering of stars in the sky. I know how brightly they shine individually. Upon retirement, however, I found myself looking for a way to connect them—to make sense of how and why mentorship succeeds, and how and why it sometimes fails. This book is my personal attempt to link those stars, to draw meaningful constellations out of the dozens of disparate stories I've been privileged to witness.

Or, put more simply: I had questions! I'm a journalist by training, and my first job was at the *Ponca City News*, my hometown newspaper in northern Oklahoma, near the Kansas border. For as long as I can remember, I've been geared toward asking questions. (One of my sons gave me a "three-questions-per day" limit during his senior year in high school because he became so tired of my inquisitiveness.)

I believe that every young person has insights, experiences, and perspectives that make them unique and valuable, and that helping all children reach their potential should be our number one societal priority. I embraced my questioning nature to revisit a few of the young adults who had "grown up" at the Memorial Park Boys & Girls Club to ask about their impressions and get their permission to share their stories. Did their Club experiences really help them thrive? And how did their relationships with staff and volunteers provide direction and hope?

I also wanted to express gratitude to God for leading me through the iconic blue doors of a Boys & Girls Club. (Blue doors are among the organization's signatures, and they're meant to signal an inclusive, safe, and welcoming place for children and teens.) It is important to note, however, that Boys & Girls Clubs of America is a secular organization. Its traditional Clubs, like the one I led before retirement, do not promote a particular way of viewing the world. References to faith in this book, therefore, relate to my personal beliefs.

This is not a self-help text, a scientific study of mentorship, or conclusive document about Boys & Girls Clubs of America as an organization. It's an exploration, an honest attempt to demonstrate how caring adults can ignite the bright potential of America's youth, creating effervescent constellations of hope. Thank you for joining me on this star-gazing journey.

Jane

CHAPTER 1
From Suicide to Strength

"The most beautiful people we have known are those who have known defeat, known suffering, known struggle, known loss, and have found their way out of the depths. These persons have an appreciation, a sensitivity, and an understanding of life that fills them with compassion, gentleness, and a deep loving concern. Beautiful people do not just happen."

—Elisabeth Kübler-Ross

JESSICA

Jessica tried to end her life, thinking it was the only way to "stop the madness."

The state had removed the preteen from her birth family to save her from her mother's physical and emotional abuse. Her father was in prison. She had not only endured her mother's attacks directly but had tried to protect her nine-, five-, and three-year-old half-siblings from the violence. All four of them became wards of the state, scattered to various temporary families.

By age eleven, Jessica entered the trauma of foster care.

By fifteen, she'd run away or been removed from thirteen foster homes and had tried to end her life.

A positive detour following her suicide attempt led Jessica to the Boys & Girls Club of Oklahoma County, where we met. I remember distinctly the first time I saw her. Each December, we asked the teens to help pack and distribute holiday goodies for the younger Club members. It was on one of those days that I spotted this beautiful girl with velvety brown skin, sparkling eyes, and a red-and-green holiday scarf wrapped around her curly black hair. The little ones gathered closely around her as she stuffed tiny toys, candy, and books into treat bags for them. They liked her warm smile and could feel her genuine interest and concern. I could see right away that she was a natural-born leader.

A few weeks after the holiday event, I saw Jessica sitting at a table in the Clubhouse lobby, making pencil sketches of an evening gown. I stopped to ask about her drawings.

"I'm entering a contest to get a scholarship to New York University," she told me. "The contest is to create and sew an original dress design, and the winner can get a full four-year scholarship."

I was impressed that Jessica was establishing goals for herself, but I also knew a college education would be a tremendous stretch for someone in her situation. By then, I'd learned that she had been failing her classes at a traditional public high school and had been transferred to an alternative school housed at a local technology center.

When asked further about the NYU competition, Jessica explained that part of the application was to sew the dress of her own design. While her foster mom owned a sewing machine, she worked long hours and was not available to take Jessica to a fabric store to buy supplies. Jessica asked me to take her, and with her foster mom's approval, we set out to find the materials needed. In the end—for various reasons—she was unable to complete the gown she had designed for the NYU challenge, but that experience gave me clear insight into the strength of Jessica's spirit and her determination to take the steps necessary to build a better life. It also created the beginning of a meaningful relationship.

I watched with joy as Jessica took on additional responsibilities at the Club. She claimed a leadership role among a group of seven- to seventeen-year-olds when we agreed to author a book for a national publisher. Called *O is for Oklahoma*, the children's book took each letter of the alphabet as a jumping off point for a photograph and short story or couplet about something important to our state.

Jessica, no surprise, took the first letter in the alphabet, dedicating it to the Arbuckle Mountains. Next to a photograph of a waterfall cascading down the side of a mountain, she wrote:

A is for Arbuckle Mountains.
Come one, come all,
and buckle down.
She roars in beauty and in sound.

Jessica's page in the book

I saw Jessica developing academically and emotionally—roaring in her own ways. Even going to high school at the tech center, which had resulted from academic disappointments, proved to be a blessing. At that alternative school, Jessica became motivated to advance at her own rate through online courses. She enjoyed the natural high that came with finishing each course and even became a tour guide and spokesperson for the school. She progressed quickly and suddenly was on track to graduate with outstanding grades a year ahead of her peers.

She found purpose in helping Club staff in the kitchen serve snacks and meals to the other kids. Having often been hungry as a child at home, she told me that it was particularly meaningful to share the sustenance of healthy food and positive times as part of a community in the lunchroom.

Prior to high school graduation, Jessica competed in the Boys & Girls Clubs of America's Youth of the Year contest, designed to recognize and honor outstanding leadership and accomplishments of Club members. The process requires each participant to write several essays about their life's challenges, their goals for the future, and how their experiences at the Boys & Girls Club shaped their young lives. It also includes preparing a three-minute speech describing the challenges they've overcome.

Jessica's willingness to share the private pain of her journey inspired the local Club competition judges, and she was selected to share her story at a patron's gala event before moving up to the state competition. A local donor contributed funds to help Jessica go with staff to shop for appropriate banquet attire and a more professional outfit for competing at the state level. She looked and felt beautiful and accomplished in her lovely dress and interview suit.

"Have any of you ever had bruises around your wrists and arms from being restrained?" Jessica asked the audience as she started her speech. She followed that rhetorical question by describing in more detail the physical and verbal abuse she had endured as a young child. She explained that her mom had told her multiple times that she wished Jessica had never been born. The sixteen-year-old shared her roller-coaster ride of painful foster home placements and chaos, but expressed gratitude that one of those placements resulted in her finding the Boys & Girls Club. That was where she found caring adults and positive activities that helped her replace despair with hope and disappointment with opportunity. Having the Boys & Girls Club to go to every day after school gave her a sense of stability, security, acceptance, and, most importantly, love.

I sat near the front of the event ballroom where Jessica shared her story with over four hundred guests. When she talked about her feelings of being completely rejected as a child, I heard audible gasps and noticed others joining me in wiping away tears. The beauty and confidence she portrayed on stage in her first fancy dress was in sharp contrast to the traumatic experiences she described.

A few days later, a panel of dignitaries—including state legislators, representatives of the governor's office, and well-known business leaders—interviewed the fifteen Youth of the Year candidates from Clubs around the state. The teens shared their personal stories of overcoming trauma, neglect, and hopelessness through involvement at their local Clubs.

While there were team-building activities for the competitors during the two-day experience, Jessica and each of the other contenders had to face a panel of judges alone on the second day. They were quizzed about their lives apart from their Boys & Girls Clubs and asked to present their three-minute prepared speeches. Jessica dressed in a tailored black pantsuit to address the prestigious judges, with her head held high and confidence beyond her years. As in the local competition, she talked about the extreme challenges of her childhood and how being an active member of the Club gave her the courage to apply herself to building a better future.

Jessica won over the statewide panel of judges, and they named her Boys & Girls Club of America's Oklahoma Youth of the Year. She shared her speech at a luncheon of state dignitaries as she was named the state's honoree. The title of Oklahoma Youth of the Year afforded her recognition and college scholarship opportunities, and qualified her for the Southwest Region competition in Dallas the following summer.

I was honored to be Jessica's staff sponsor to the three-day regional competition. It was interesting to watch her interact with Club kids from other states, striving to find commonalities and differences. In fact, she became so focused on being with the others that I had a hard time tracking her down some of the time. I was intent on helping her practice her speech to make a good impression, but she was more interested in developing friendships. Each of the eight Youths of the Year chosen to represent their respective states had risen above challenging, often abusive childhoods to create their own pathways to success. Their stories were painful and unfair, but not unusual.

Jessica was a finalist in the Southwest Region's competition, second only to the young woman who was subsequently named the national Boys & Girls Clubs of America (BGCA) Youth of the Year. Advancing to that level provided Jessica multiple life-giving opportunities, including the ability to speak before an audience of more than a thousand business and community leaders—including Jim Clark, the president of Boys & Girls Clubs of America. Beyond that, it resulted in significant scholarship money that made it possible for her to continue her education. Exhausted from the stress of the competition and staying up until wee-hours of the morning with her new friends, Jessica fell fast asleep on the backseat of my car and remained there without a word for the three-and-a-half-hour ride back from Dallas.

The glow of graduating from high school and competing in BGCA's regional Youth of the Year process faded quickly, though, after Jessica returned to Oklahoma. While she was rising to heights of recognition and success, she arrived home to find her father looking for ways to stymie her independence and control her life.

I remember the day Jessica told me that her dad was being released from prison and that she was afraid that the Department of Human Services would make her move in with him. She barely knew him, and court records showed that he had multiple convictions of possession and distribution of federally controlled dangerous substances, vehicle theft, and domestic abuse. She had been feeling secure in her current foster home and didn't understand why she needed to move just before high school graduation.

Her fears became reality. The state required Jessica and her younger brother to move with their dad to a government-subsidized apartment her senior year in high school. She told me he was not physically abusive, but she was still not comfortable living with him. He regularly called her into his bedroom in the middle of the night and demanded that she bring him a sandwich or something to drink. She and her little brother supported each other by cooking their own meals, walking to the bus stop to get to school while their dad was sleeping, and spending free time at the Boys & Girls Club and a nearby library to do homework and feel safe.

Perhaps most alarmingly, Jessica's dad became a significant roadblock to the future she was working hard to create. She told me that he controlled and monopolized the state payments intended to help support her yet did not use the funds for her benefit. Her father did not have a valid driver's license or functioning vehicle and refused to help her attain her own driver's license (a necessity in a city with limited public transportation). Through her own initiative, Jessica obtained a permit and enrolled at a local driver's education course to get her license. She had graduated from high school at age sixteen with an excellent grade point average and was accepted at the University of Central Oklahoma, but her father refused to sign paperwork necessary to move forward in her enrollment process. He threatened to report her as a runaway when she attended events at the university.

Refusing to allow her father's unyielding efforts to obstruct her progress, at sixteen years old, Jessica sought to become legally emancipated from her parents. She wanted to start her adult life without legal ties to her troubled past and took the initiative to free herself from her father's selfish restraints. Her mother quickly signed the paperwork, reiterating that she had never wanted her. Her dad, however, fought the emancipation and was held in contempt of court by the judge for yelling during proceedings, she said. The judge ruled in Jessica's favor in 2013. The state sent her younger brother back to live with their mom, and Jessica went to live with a Boys & Girls Club supporter until she could move into a college dormitory the next fall.

Completely on her own, Jessica started her collegiate career at the University of Central Oklahoma in Edmond before transferring as a sophomore to the University of Oklahoma (OU), an hour away. Many first-generation college students, even those with family support, struggle to adapt to a university environment and maintain their focus and drive long enough to graduate. According to the national Center for First Generation Student Success, students who are the first in their families to attend college make up a third of all college students, but only twenty-seven percent of them attain their degrees within four years—markedly lagging peers who had one or two parents with college degrees.

Beating the odds once again, Jessica persevered. She took part-time jobs around campus and continually sought additional scholarships. With the help of financial aid, the support of mentors, and her own dedication and resiliency, in 2018, Jessica graduated with a bachelor's degree in human relations.

On graduation night, I nervously looked through the bustling crowd for Jessica's boyfriend, Juan, who had sent me a text that he was saving us seats. I had butterflies in my stomach as I thought about how many obstacles this young woman had faced before walking across the stage at the Lloyd Noble Center Arena in her black graduation cap and gown. She would be accepting her diploma and changing the trajectory of her life for the better, and I was certain that no one in that eleven-thousand-seat arena on that cold December evening deserved the honor more.

I was relieved to find Juan in the bleachers and surprised to see the person sitting next to him... Jessica's mother! It warmed my heart to realize that despite their past troubled relationship, Jessica had invited her mom to attend her graduation. When I asked her about it later, she said she wanted to be able to stay connected with her younger siblings and recognized that her struggles with her mom were consequences of mental illness. She had forgiven her for the years of physical and emotional abuse. Jessica's mom jumped up and down in the bleachers, cheering loudly for her daughter in what appeared to me to be a beautiful story of redemption.

CREATING A DIFFERENT KIND OF FAMILY

Jessica met Juan on a dating app during her time at OU. They met up for their first in-person date outside a Bass Pro Shop, then wandered around Oklahoma City's historic Bricktown (a charming downtown district with a canal and brick-lined streets) for a couple of hours before deciding to eat at a local pizza shop. Juan gave her a type of unconditional and supportive love she had never experienced. He quickly became the love of her life. He worked as an auto mechanic for a local car dealership and was part of a large, supportive family who welcomed Jessica into their fold.

The happy couple

The fall following her graduation, Juan and Jessica spoke loving words of commitment as husband and wife under a giant canopy of elm trees at a private wedding venue in the country. Jessica looked stunning in her long white wedding gown and veil. Juan was dashing in his black tuxedo with gold vest and bow tie. Close family and a small group of friends gathered to celebrate the ceremony held on a wooden outdoor stage, with a local preacher officiating as the couple shared their vows.

My family was blessed to be three of their thirty invited guests, and the love in the air was palpable. Following the ceremony, we enjoyed a fabulous feast of the family's homemade enchiladas, tortillas, and wedding cake.

When my family reconnected with Jessica and Juan at a large city park over four years later, it was clear on that cool, bright and sunny day, that Jessica was still in a good place. Juan and their three-year-old son walked hand-in-hand while their two-year-old daughter enjoyed a lofty view of her surroundings from a child carrier backpack on her mom's back. They told us then that their family was looking forward to the arrival of baby number three the following summer.

Jessica stays at home with their children and plans to homeschool them, dedicating herself to their happiness and growth. When I visited their home, I saw bookshelves brimming with colorful educational and entertaining books and interactive learning toys occupying spaces throughout. She told me she had started researching the materials she will need to continue to provide a robust learning environment as they become school aged.

By all accounts, Jessica is an exceptional mother. She takes the kids to local libraries and area parks multiple times each week. During summers, they engage in summer reading challenges from two libraries. They don't have far to go for nature lessons, as the family grows vegetables of all kinds in their backyard, and the parents use the gardens as living classrooms to teach their children the value of hard work and fresh foods.

She continues to surpass my high expectations in many facets of her life, including taking multiple online classes to become an authority in horticulture and entomology. She loves to share stories about the various insects that harm or help certain plants, how to grow plants without pesticides, what species attract butterflies, and other mysteries of nature. The area Conservation District has named her family as members of their Community Resiliency Project. One evening, she and Juan invited my family to tour their gardens and enjoy a delicious dinner made mostly of vegetables they had grown. It made me think back to Jessica's comments years earlier, about how she had first found comfort and security at the Boys & Girls Club by helping staff serve healthy meals and snacks in the Club kitchen.

Understanding firsthand the impact that early trauma can cause, Jessica has become dedicated to promoting efforts to ensure that all babies and toddlers have the resources they need to thrive. Jessica and Juan are members of Zero to Three, a national organization whose mission is to ensure that all children have a strong start in life and the ability to reach their full potential.

Demonstrating her customary fortitude and leadership, Jessica recently applied to the organization to obtain a scholarship for the whole family to travel to Washington, DC, to advocate for support of quality and affordable childcare. While there, they joined families from forty-nine other states to meet with members of their Congressional delegations and legislative leaders. I was thrilled when she texted to me photos of her family with Secretary of Transportation Pete Buttigieg and former Speaker of the US House of Representatives Nancy Pelosi. When they returned, she and Juan told me about their meetings with staff in the Congressional delegation's offices. While the bill they were supporting for affordable childcare was seen as a "Democrat's" bill, they believed that it also aligned with Republican members' pro-life stance. After demonstrating her advocacy skills, Zero to Three hired Jessica as head captain of Family Support.

Jessica is not only interested in breaking the cycle of trauma and abuse in her own family but also in becoming a resource for other families with young children. It is astonishing that this young woman, who had experienced horrific abuse and rejection, could rise above the challenges of her younger life to invest not only in herself and her family but in efforts to help children everywhere get a better start in life.

Jessica credits her exposure to positive role models and mentors, as well as enriching experiences such as college tours, writing *O is for Oklahoma*, meeting kids from other states with similar stories, and participating in an art/science program at the Boys & Girls Club, for giving her the confidence to build a life of promise for herself, her family, and the larger community. She has found purpose and meaning as a dedicated wife, mother, teacher, and advocate… miraculously shattering a multigenerational cycle of poverty and abuse. At only twenty-six years old, Jessica is already creating a beautiful legacy for a new generation.

CHAPTER 2
Just Three Caring Women

"Never doubt that a small group of thoughtful, committed citizens can change the world. Indeed, it is the only thing that ever has."

—Margaret Mead

An American cultural anthropologist with acclaim in the 1960s and '70s, Margaret Mead helped shed light on the influential power of small groups of people who are galvanized around a shared purpose. Her words are often cited to inspire others to act.

A century before Mead's time, Boys & Girls Clubs of America had its simple beginnings in 1860 in Hartford, Connecticut, when three women, Mary Goodwin, Alice Goodwin, and Elizabeth Hammersley, saw a problem. They noticed a challenge for families of many immigrant workers in the factories and mills that were popping up during the Industrial Revolution. Their children sometimes worked as "clinker boys," shoveling hot bricks into kilns. After work, their fathers often headed to the local bars, leaving the boys to wander the streets.

Believing that these boys deserved better options and opportunities, the three women organized a club they called the Goodwill Club. They invited the children into their homes for snacks and structured activities, and focused on capturing the boys' interests, improving their behavior, and increasing their personal expectations and goals. A movement was born. It planted the seeds for the organization I would join a century and one-half later.

A decade after the Hartford women started the Goodwill Club, a man named John Collins formed a similar club in another burgeoning industrial hub, New York City. Collins is said to have established three principles that have guided the organization for over a century:
1. It was okay to play games, but the boys must follow rules.
2. The club was for all boys, regardless of religion.
3. The priority was for the club to serve impoverished boys.

Collin's focus was on physical, mental, and moral development. In today's BGCA lingo, these assets are referred to as "healthy lifestyles," "academic success," and "good character and citizenship." The Club was founded on the belief that a positive environment would bring out the best traits of a child. Today, this is referred to as the "Club experience."

Similar Clubs started springing up in the eastern part of the United States. In 1906, fifty-three organizations came together to establish a strong central organization that could provide support and direction to local clubs, and created the Federated Boys' Clubs. Then, in 1931, with the help of President Herbert Hoover, the organization became the Boys Clubs of America. As the predecessors to what became the Boys & Girls Club movement found purpose in the chaos of the Industrial Revolution, another historical event contributed to the organization's growth in the mid-1900s: World War II. With the rise of women in the workforce during and after World War II, more and more mothers started working outside the home and needed safe places for their children to be after school. In 1956, the organization received a Congressional Charter, a law passed by Congress that states the mission, authority, and activities of a group and lends it legitimacy as being officially sanctioned by the US government.

Girls started attending Boys Clubs as well. By the 1970s and '80s, most Clubs served an even mix of girls and boys, and in 1990, the organization officially changed its name to Boys & Girls Clubs of America.

The need to address the challenges of our country's youth has grown exponentially since the three women in Hartford, Connecticut, made a commitment to those wayward boys on the streets. While the Industrial Revolution and World War II motivated early Club organizers, today our society is faced with a host of social issues of similar magnitude and effect: police violence, school shootings, longstanding opportunity gaps, racial discrimination, and lingering mental health issues following a global pandemic, to name a few. The good news is that increasing numbers of communities are seeing Boys & Girls Clubs as a key ingredient for making society more equitable and helping children and teens thrive amid these serious challenges.

> In 2020, firearms became the leading cause of death of children and teens in our country, a notorious place long-held by automobile accidents.
>
> The devastation of school gun violence is like a tsunami, drowning the innocence of school-aged children everywhere. Teachers, students, and parents all fear the possibility of horrific violence within school walls. Active shooter drills have become routine in school districts through-out the country.

Today, there are 11,089 Boys & Girls Club programs operating in our fifty states and military bases, serving 4.5 million kids in over five thousand Clubhouses. Other Clubs are held in schools, churches, government housing, and community centers. For more than 160 years, Boys & Girls Clubs have been known as a second home for generations of Americans, providing more than forty-million youth with mentors, meals, and meaningful life experiences. Clubs are anchors in their communities: allies to schools, partners to parents, and springboards of potential for kids and teens.

The list of well-known successful people who have come through the blue doors of a Boys Club or a Boys & Girls Club attests to the organization's positive association with children who have reached unthinkable potential. Among them are General Wesley Clark, Misty Copeland, Cuba Gooding Jr., Magic Johnson, Jennifer Lopez, Shaquille O'Neil, Sugar Ray Leonard, Katy Perry, Adam Sandler,

Usher, and Denzel Washington. How did these people, like my mentee Jessica, capture that spark—some sort of boost—that helped propel them into adulthood?

All Boys & Girls Clubs in the country share the same mission: "to inspire and enable all youth, especially those who need us most, to reach their full potential as productive, caring, and responsible citizens." The accompanying vision is "to provide a world-class Club experience that assures success is within reach of every young person who enters our doors, with all members on track to graduate from high school with a plan for the future, demonstrating good character and citizenship, and living a healthy lifestyle."

In today's environment of kids being bullied, discounted, or shamed due to the color of their skin, sexual identity, gender orientation, socio-economic status, or religion, BGCA's published and lived commitment to full inclusiveness is particularly important. If we believe that they are all our kids and that each one deserves a chance to reach their potential, then society can't pick and choose whom to nurture and whom to disregard.

How do these 11,089 programs around the country help kids with all kinds of backgrounds and challenges realize their potential? Clubs follow a formula for affecting positive change called the Formula for Impact:

> BGCA data compares national averages of the general youth population with children and teens who regularly attend a Club. Obtained from a national anonymous survey of kids and teens ages nine to eighteen, results demonstrate that Club kids have higher graduation rates, better grades, increased interest in science, technology, engineering, and math-related careers, greater likelihood of volunteering in the community, and greater self-esteem.
>
> Today's Club youth responded that they are committed to societal change and passionate about social justice issues that continue to top headlines. Eighty-two percent of the youth indicated that they believe they can make a difference in their community. More than half of the teens identified racial justice as the top social issue they most care about. Interestingly, social justice was the number one social issue for kids from each of the racial categories represented.

Just Three Caring Women

The Youth Who Need Us Most
(low-income, lacking supervision or accessible opportunities)
+
Outcome-Driven Club Experiences
(safe place, fun, recognition, relationships, opportunities, and expectations)
+
High-Yield Activities (fun with a purpose), Targeted Programs (evidence-based), and Regular Attendance
=
Academic Success, Healthy Lifestyles, and Good Character and Citizenship

CENTRAL OKLAHOMA YOUTH

In 1950, nearly one hundred years after the three caring women in Connecticut established the Goodwill Club and launched a movement, the Central Oklahoma Salvation Army formed the first Boys Club in Oklahoma City. BGCA issues charters for Club organizations in three categories: Salvation Army, Native American, and Traditional. The distinctions relate primarily to the type of governance of the serving organization (and Salvation Army Clubs include a Christian component).

A few men who had been involved with the Salvation Army Club in downtown Oklahoma City saw a need to reach more youth in the community. They led the charge for expansion by asking BGCA to grant them permission to charter a traditional Club organization. There was a fifty-member minimum to start a Club in those days, so the founders signed up their kids and neighbors' kids to get things started. In 1995, BGCA approved the charter for the Boys & Girls Clubs of Oklahoma County. It was in that Club organization that I found my home sixteen years later.

The visionary founders looked for a Clubhouse location that would draw kids from nearby neighborhoods and schools in an unserved area of town. Memorial Park, one of the oldest and most beloved city parks in near-northwest Oklahoma City, offered a rarely used Kiwanis community center building that seemed an ideal location for Club activities. The national Kiwanis organization had ties to BGCA and older Clubs around the country, and the local chapter welcomed establishment of a new Boys & Girls Club in their building.

At the time, there were concerns about illegal and potentially dangerous gang activity in the inner-city park, but once positive things started happening with kids there during the day, the nefarious elements seemed to disperse. Concerns about possible graffiti, drug use, and other related problems did not materialize.

In just one year, the Boys & Girls Clubs of Oklahoma County grew to three-hundred members, five full-time and several part-time staff, a twenty-five-member board of community leaders, and an annual budget of $156,000. That small community center building was already bursting at the seams, and staff were relying on decent weather to be able to conduct activities outside in the park.

A key progress point came in 2004 when the Boys & Girls Clubs of Oklahoma County Board of Directors began a Campaign for Kids to raise funds to build a new, much larger Clubhouse to serve more youth. The next year, the organization expanded its reach with the first phase of its flagship Memorial Park Clubhouse, which included a double-court gymnasium and kitchen facility. Having an indoor gym allowed the Club to host more sports opportunities in all kinds of weather. The kitchen provided the ability to partner with the local food bank to offer meals and snacks approved by the US Food and Drug Administration.

The Club still needed more classroom space, so construction on the second phase of the building began in 2008 and it opened its doors in 2010. That phase completed the thirty-five-thousand-square-foot Clubhouse and accommodated more than twice as many Club members as the small Kiwanis Club building. It also provided separate areas for the teens and younger kids, and created multiple classroom spaces, allowing the Club to expand the variety and depth of their programming.

The Memorial Park Boys & Girls Club

The large Clubhouse faced a well-traveled street in the popular park in the heart of the city, which gave the Club more visibility and community recognition. Awareness was important not only so parents would know about the Club's availability for their children but also to acquaint members of the public with the need for and purpose of the organization.

Just as the doors to the expanded Clubhouse opened for the first time, the doors of my longtime career in local government were slamming shut. Little did I know, as I passed the advancing construction on the way to my Bricktown office, that the big red brick building with the iconic Boys & Girls Clubs blue knuckles over the front doors would soon become my daily destination. Also unimaginable at the time was how the trajectory of the organization would take off from those simple beginnings at one building site to eighteen locations and over sixteen thousand local Club members.

CHAPTER 3
The Universal Language of Hope

"If we want to enrich the transmission of humane, compassionate beliefs and practices, and minimize the transmission of hateful, destructive beliefs, we need to be very mindful of what we're exposing our children to. Are they spending time with people who are different from them? Are they seeing diversity celebrated? Or are they being raised to fear and judge anyone who doesn't think or look or speak like they do?"

—Bruce D. Perry, *What Happened to You?*

SERGIO

Sergio's mom moved with her husband from Mexico to Oklahoma City just a couple of months before he was born. Soon after, his dad abandoned the family, leaving her to provide for her two little girls, eight and four years old, along with their new baby brother.

Speaking only Spanish, Sergio's mom loved her children and did her best to provide for their needs by flipping hamburgers at McDonald's and working as a hostess at Poblano Grill (a Mexican restaurant). But her income from two jobs barely put food on the table, and there was no one to help with her three young children. The girls had attended school in Mexico, but because their mom was working seventeen-hour days and unable to provide transportation, they weren't going to school in the US. Instead of learning to read and write and making friends, Sergio's young sisters were left changing diapers, fixing bottles, and comforting their baby brother when he cried.

A co-worker at Poblano Grill was fluent in Spanish and befriended Sergio's struggling mom. When he realized that the two little girls were left at home to care for their baby brother instead of going to school, he told his parents about his friend's desperate situation. After hearing the story, his parents offered to adopt the two little girls, then ten and six years old. The couple had recently lost a son in a car accident and felt called to welcome the girls into their family. They promised the girls' mom that they would support their academic, emotional, and physical growth while remaining in regular contact with Sergio and her. She agreed to the adoption while keeping two-year-old Sergio by her side.

The toddler's cramped, one-bedroom apartment sat in a neighborhood known for gang activity and drive-by shootings. Window shades were drawn to remain under the radar. There were few toys and little space to play inside, and the rusty, dilapidated playground equipment next to the complex was a magnet for predators. Sergio was not allowed to go outside. He had no friends to play with or adults who could help him learn English.

In that season of desperation, Sergio's mom could have never imagined that her son would later graduate with honors from one of the most prestigious high schools in the state and accept a full-ride scholarship to a nationally renowned university. The first glimmer of hope—and the ultimate realization of that unimagined dream—began when his mom found the Boys & Girls Club.

Five-year-old Sergio was shy and physically shaking the first time he walked into the Club. He didn't know anyone, hadn't started school, and didn't speak a word of English, but the foosball and pool tables did catch his eye. A master of speaking the "language of all kids," senior staff member A.Jaye Johnson greeted Sergio at the front door and immediately created a bond to last a lifetime.

A.Jaye took the frightened child back to the kitchen to get some scrambled eggs, sausage, and orange juice, and introduced him to other kids his age. He made sure all the staff knew that Sergio would need help with his language skills. They found books written in Spanish in the Club library to teach him the corresponding English words. They involved Spanish-speaking staff members when necessary to ensure thorough communication.

When I met Sergio three years later, at eight years old, he had gotten more fluent in English but remained quiet and timid. He was a slim little boy who was usually found close on the heels of his mentor, A.Jaye. When I reconnected with the twenty-two-year-old Sergio recently, he reminded me of how frightening those early days were for him, without having command of the English language, and what a difference it had made in his life to have a staff mentor to shepherd his growth.

Sergio told me that kids and staff at the Club had assumed that with his Hispanic heritage, he would want to play soccer, but he had always wanted to play basketball. He loved shooting hoops and running up and down the court with the other kids, staff, and volunteers in the gym. He said he relished the Club's relationship with the Oklahoma City Thunder NBA team and grew to really love everything about the basketball culture… the players, the teams, and their schedules.

In fact, the Thunder Cares organization gave Sergio his first bicycle at a Thunder game on Christmas Day his first year at the Club. He was thrilled to meet Desmond Mason, Russell Westbrook, and Kevin Durant in person. A few years later, he was privileged to attend Durant's MVP awards ceremony with a group of kids and staff, where they each received the cool KD backpack that Sergio constantly wore throughout high school. He said the Thanksgiving Dinner at the Club sponsored by Westbrook's Why Not Foundation and the United Way was the first such holiday dinner his family had experienced. His mom won a turkey at the event raffle that first year and, with the recipe provided, learned to bake a turkey—a skill she has used every Thanksgiving since.

Sergio had a built-in group of tutors at the Club, ensuring that he had the help he needed to do his school assignments. If the language barrier made communication with a teacher difficult, A.Jaye called the school to resolve any misunderstandings. Support with his schoolwork later paid off when he took a chance to apply to a highly ranked, competitive public middle and high school with rigorous admission policies. The basketball coach at the school was a volunteer coach at the Boys & Girls Club and encouraged Sergio to apply.

A CLOSE CALL

I asked Sergio how that shy little boy had evolved into a teenager who was willing to take such a risk to apply, and I was somewhat alarmed when he responded that his propensity for risk-taking had appeared early on at the Club. He admitted that he had nearly drowned during a Club outing to a large public swimming pool. Safety is, of course, the overarching priority of all Boys & Girls Clubs and was always top of mind for me as the CEO. There are, however, inherent risks when offering a wide variety of fun experiences for kids, including summer swimming.

Sergio explained that his first ever "trip" was a Club outing to the local pool. When he learned that the field trip cost a dollar, he quickly ran out to the park behind the Club and scavenged four quarters from the bottom of the park's iconic fountain. He was wearing basketball shorts, which doubled as a swim suit. The trip to the water park was a whole new adventure.

The five-year-old, whose mom had kept him inside their apartment to avoid dangers in their neighborhood, was particularly fascinated by the giant slide at the deep end of the swimming pool and immediately ran in that direction. The only problem was… *he couldn't swim!* At lunch with me years later, he laughed as he described going down that slide, landing in the pool with a splash, sinking to the bottom, and beginning to drown before the lifeguard jumped in to rescue him! He said Club staff had asked him earlier if he could swim, but because his English was so limited, he didn't really understand what they were asking and had just nodded as a learned response. Sometimes saving a life requires an actual lifeguard.

That risk at the pool worked out, as did the risk to apply to Classen School of Advanced Studies for middle and high school. In high school, Sergio continued to excel academically and began to accept more leadership roles within the Club. He became the president of the Keystone Club, an elite group of high schoolers who dedicate some of their free time to serving in the community.

After seeing people rummage through the trash dumpsters in the park looking for food at the end of the day, Keystone teens built a four-shelf wooden food pantry outside the Clubhouse. They stocked the pantry, painted blue with bright yellow and orange flowers, with non-perishable food. They also included Starbursts and a few other fun treats they liked and wanted to share. Members of the local homeless community cleaned out the pantry day after day.

Following hurricane disasters in Houston, Texas, Sergio and fellow Keystone members sacrificed their spring break to help rebuild a Boys & Girls Club severely damaged by the storms. What they didn't have in carpentry skills, they made up for with energy, enthusiasm, and empathy for their peers in another state.

Keystone planned and conducted a Career Fair for metro-area high school students. The Career Fair introduced Club members and other area teens to various future work opportunities that they otherwise may never had considered as possibilities. Keystone members learned valuable planning and outreach lessons by recruiting representatives of local businesses and nearby colleges and universities to share information at the fair.

Sergio also was involved in local and out-of-state college visits through the Club, beginning fortuitously with a visit to Oklahoma City University (OCU) as a sixth grader. Other colleges he visited with his Keystone friends included the University of Kansas, Colorado State University, Colorado University at Boulder, Georgia State University, Howard University, Full Sail University, Memphis State University, and closer to home, the University of Oklahoma, Oklahoma State University, Oklahoma Christian University, and the University of Central Oklahoma.

Sergio's leadership in Keystone led to his being hired as a junior staff member during his sophomore year in high school. His first role as a Boys & Girls Club employee was to help longtime staff member Sharon Gordon Linton in the kindergarten classroom. Sergio had known Sharon since his first days as a timid Club kid, and he enjoyed helping her with the youngest members. He told me when we met recently that he was excited that his little brother followed his footsteps as a junior staff member and had the opportunity to work with Sharon as well.

Receiving his first paycheck created a dilemma for Sergio, however. He did not have a bank account in which to deposit his check, nor did his mom. A.Jaye took him to the bank, where they opened a joint account, which he still has today. His lifelong mentor also helped him shop for his first suit and found professionals who were willing to donate their services to test and fit him with eye glasses and braces to straighten his teeth, all of which boosted the enterprising teen's confidence.

The following year, a new Club site opened in a Hispanic area of the community, and we asked Sergio to provide support for staff, kids, and parents at that location. With the ability to communicate well with the parents who had limited English, his success there led to even more responsibility as the organization opened other Clubs with predominately Hispanic populations. He said when conflicts arose, he learned that a nonjudgmental listening ear could turn things around. In his car, Sergio kept artwork drawn by the kids as a constant reminder of how important it was to help them feel good about themselves.

His senior year coincided with the eightieth anniversary of the superhero Batman, and to recognize that milestone, BGCA awarded Sergio a Batman Award for his determination, bravery, and leadership. He was honored at a Saturday Fun Day in the Club gymnasium, with a special visit by a local Batman impersonator. *Metro Families*, an area magazine, highlighted Sergio in its Super Kids of the Metro Series, calling him a Community Crusader.

A. Jaye Johnson, Jane Sutter, and Sergio

The Memorial Park Boys & Girls Clubs named Sergio as its Youth of the Year, and he, like Jessica, was subsequently named Youth of the Year for the State of Oklahoma. Also being named a Clara Luper Scholar at OCU, which provides full tuition for four years, accentuated his growing success. He had previously thought he would go to the University of Kansas after the college visit there, but he valued the significant scholarship that OCU offered, and as the time neared, he realized that he wanted to stay closer to home to be available for his mom, two younger brothers, and a girlfriend, who still had one more year in high school.

I wasn't sure how Sergio would feel about reconnecting with me four years later, but I was pleasantly surprised with how quickly and affirmatively he answered my text inviting him to coffee or lunch. When we met at a restaurant near his university, I was impressed with how handsome he looked and how confident and mature he sounded.

He told me that things had gotten tough for him after high school graduation in the spring of 2020, the height of the COVID pandemic. That unfortunate timing resulted in multiple lost opportunities. He was chosen to be a Bank of America Intern, but because of the pandemic, none of the interns were allowed to travel to a national gathering of interns in Washington, DC, as they had done in previous years. Regional gatherings of Boys & Girls Clubs' Youths of the Year were canceled, resulting in a missed opportunity to represent as his state's Youth of the Year or meet other outstanding students from the Southwest Region. The cancellation of that event also resulted in reduced availability of BGCA scholarships.

ANOTHER CLOSE CALL

Sergio told me that the pandemic cloud had continued to hang over his head his freshman year at OCU. The future had been looking bright following his twelve years at the Boys & Girls Club and academic success in a rigorous high school environment, but being a first-generation college student in a pandemic lockdown presented additional challenges and disappointments. While still allowed to live in a dorm on campus, having to take most of his classes online and suffering limited interaction with professors and other students due to strict pandemic measures took a real toll.

Sergio told me that depression and lack of focus had played havoc with his grades, and he was put on probation with his scholarship. He considered changing colleges, but like the lifeguard who saved him from drowning in the swimming pool years earlier, a capable and encouraging academic advisor saved him from drowning at OCU. The advisor provided a grace period for him to bring his grade point up to the required 3.0. Sergio said he is proud of himself for becoming more conscious of his decisions and their consequences and doing what it took to slowly redeem his academic status to maintain the scholarship. He laughed when he told me that, during his most recent semester as a junior, he had "coasted" through his classes to end up with a 3.86 semester average.

LOOKING AT THE BOYS & GIRLS CLUB THROUGH A FAMILY LENS

In exploring and questioning the impact of Boys & Girls Clubs, my recent conversation with Sergio as a young adult caused me to consider the effect of the Club in a new way—not only on children but whole families. While I had been amazed at the transformations I had seen among children, I had given only superficial consideration to the ways Boys & Girls Clubs serve and shape struggling families.

"I had a really good childhood because of the Boys & Girls Club," Sergio told me. "It allowed me to enjoy being a kid, but the impact was even greater for my mom. I don't think people realize how difficult it is for families to survive without support. My mom was working two jobs and needed a safe place for me to be while she worked to create a better life for our family. My sisters had given up much of their childhoods to stay home to take care of me when I was a baby."

He talked about how his older sisters had been forced to grow up too quickly as caretakers before they were adopted. Even though his sisters moved with their adoptive family to Wyoming, Sergio was quick to share how things worked out well because the adopting parents made sure the girls visited Oklahoma City every summer and the two families spend holidays together. With the adoptive parents' support, the girls made up for lost time in school, and both have since graduated from college. They consider themselves one big extended family and are in regular contact with Sergio, his mom, and two younger brothers.

What role did the Boys & Girls Club play in nurturing this struggling family?

"Without the Boys & Girls Club, I wouldn't be finishing college and I wouldn't be helping my younger brother complete college applications. The Boys & Girls Club opened the door to the world for my whole family," he said.

CHAPTER 4
Rejection Opens the Door to Vision and Purpose

"Vision without action is merely a dream. Action without vision just passes the time. Vision with action can change the world."

—Joel A. Barker

My journey to the Boys & Girls Clubs was anything but smooth or predictable. It began with one of the worst days of my life, when my longtime career came to a screeching halt.

It wasn't just a job to me; it was more like a calling. For thirty years, I'd gotten up before dawn Monday through Friday and headed to work at the Association of Central Oklahoma Governments (ACOG) as part of a team, with a boss I admired and respected.

I had clear goals and believed my contributions were valued. We made a tangible difference in the city's sprawling metro area, helping install its first regional 9-1-1 emergency phone system and working to improve water and air quality among other meaningful activities. I was part of a rich community of dedicated civic leaders. My office in Oklahoma City's Bricktown was spacious and inviting, with giant windows stretching to twenty-foot-high ceilings and overlooking streets alive with people coming and going—a constant reminder of our mission to improve life for the people who lived in the city and metropolitan area I loved.

Then, without notice, on a perfect spring day, the newly appointed director called me into his office to tell me he had eliminated my position as deputy director of the organization.

"We will have contract work for you," he said assuredly, "but wouldn't you like to kick back and relax?"

Bells went off in my head. *What?! No!* I didn't want to kick back and relax, and no, I wasn't interested in doing contract work for a person who had deemed me unessential, unnecessary, and unworthy. I told the new director that at fifty-seven I wasn't old enough to retire. I still possessed talents to contribute to the professional world. I had worked there since I was twenty-seven years old and held a wealth of institutional knowledge. Still reeling, I asked how he planned to compensate me for thirty years of dedication. There was no response.

On this day of sudden dismissal, I was lost. How was I supposed to begin a new career at this age? I had an undergraduate degree in journalism and master's in education, but my practical career experiences were in building community coalitions.

Underlying my feelings of shock and loss was grief over the death of my longtime mentor and friend two years earlier. Zach Taylor had run ACOG with exceptional skill, and I had worked alongside him to create a better regional community for our thirty-four cities, towns, and counties. The organization's priorities had shifted after his sudden death at age sixty. I had initially turned down the position of interim director because I felt grief-stricken. Two years later, the new director was showing me the door. His vision didn't match Zach's.

No longer did those in charge think it was necessary to be present in the same way to engage with the regional community. Outreach to member local governments took on a more administrative, less personal approach. Relationships were neglected. I wanted to carry on the cultural legacy that Zach and I had created, so I felt stuck in an organization that had suddenly turned internally-focused.[1]

Being cast out by Zach's replacement inflicted an immediate sense of lost self. Who was I without that role? What would I do with my days? And what about the legacy of regional unity we had created together? Then, there were the more pragmatic thoughts. Honestly, I was a lousy housekeeper and cook, so trading in my work clothes for

---

1 Leadership has since changed.

Rejection Opens the Door to Vision and Purpose

yoga pants and an apron wasn't a satisfactory option. Plus, I valued the ability to add to our family's finances.

Grief and confusion overwhelmed my heart.

While food doesn't actually resolve emotional trauma, it was lunchtime and I was eager to distance myself from what had just happened. So, I escaped to the congested sidewalks downtown. I walked past the high-rise banks and energy buildings, beyond the purple penguin statue in front of the Hallmark store, and around the corner toward a local sandwich shop.

The concrete walkway was bustling with men and women in business suits carrying briefcases, scurrying to meet a friend for lunch, rushing to the next meeting, or finishing a quick errand. If they even noticed me, they probably wondered about the crazy woman walking aimlessly and praying aloud in exasperation.

"What do you want me to do now, God? This is what I've always done!"

Suddenly, a vivid scene flashed through my brain, stopping me in my tracks. It was as clear a sight as I have ever seen or felt. Children of various ages and ethnicities filled my mind's eye. They were running, jumping, laughing, and shouting with joy. I was nowhere near a city park, and there were no children nearby. Yet, I saw them. Not only that, but I felt their energy and unbridled zest for life.

"Seriously, God?" I wondered aloud, shaking my head and feeling distinctly unsettled. What was that? Was it supposed to mean something? My mind, as usual, was flooded with questions. I thought about my experience as a student teacher three decades earlier, but the vision didn't look anything like high school journalism classes I'd taught—or like my own experience as a student. Does God still give out visions, and if so, what did this one mean? The Bible is full of them—but in the twenty-first century, and to a Presbyterian?

If this vision was an answer to my prayer, it was a perplexing one.

I continued for weeks to be frozen by the loss of my identity and purpose. I was ending a career to which I had dedicated more than half my life. Although I was given weeks to dismantle the position, even after days of sorting, sharing information with co-workers, and making necessary farewell calls and visits, stacks of books and papers to be distributed, filed, or trashed remained.

I was never one to shirk responsibilities, but I was completely undone by the process of sorting through a thirty-year career. The daily weight of it was too much. Thankfully, a co-worker and friend offered to clean up the physical mess of my office so that I could walk out of that building, and that part of my life, for good. The emotional mess would take longer to sort.

There's a grieving process when one changes jobs, particularly when the change is initiated by someone else. In my case, this included personal sorrow over the loss of my longtime mentor, boss, and friend. In a more professional sense, it involved relinquishing the ideals, values, and culture we had worked together to instill in the organization. Farewells to many co-workers and dedicated elected officials were painful. They had been such champions for progress in our metropolitan area. We shared a strong loyalty to our common purpose and, in some ways, saying goodbye felt like I was abandoning the cause.

My journalistic training had served me well in my various roles at ACOG, as I could use my communication skills to share information with local leadership and the public about often complicated regional government issues. Public safety, transportation, water quality, and economic development challenges all cross city, town, and county boundaries and are most effectively dealt with at a regional level. In Central Oklahoma, that involved coordination with over thirty mayors, council members, and county commissioners from a four-county area: not an easy task. When I told my husband of thirty-seven years that I was leaving my thirty-year career, he was quick to remind me of my talents and skills and reassure me that my compassionate heart would lead me in the right direction toward a new purpose.

I had pride in my work accomplishments, but when I searched deeply within for the moments that had brought me the most joy, I realized they were opportunities I had had as a volunteer. Zach's mentorship as a boss had reached beyond the day-to-day of our work at hand and opened a myriad of doors for me over the years, encouraging a legacy of service. The most forward-reaching gift was the space to volunteer as a mentor for children in Oklahoma City Public Schools.

When I led a group of twenty-five ACOG employees to become pen-pals with a class of third graders in a local elementary school, a beautiful, bright-eyed, and intelligent brown-skinned eight-year-old named Alecia found her way into my heart. She told me years later that the best thing she learned from our time together was a love for reading—a passion and skill that catapulted her into successful adulthood instead of generational poverty.

As I was still analyzing those memories for direction, a longtime friend and fellow church member provided a real boost. His encouragement warmed my searching heart and reignited my self-confidence. As one of Zach's closest friends, Mike Mize was familiar with my work at ACOG. He was a principal partner in a well-known and respected architectural firm and approached me about a position. I would be working on communications with the City of Oklahoma City, implementing an innovative series of projects approved by its citizens to enhance the City's infrastructure and attractiveness.

My years at ACOG and positive professional relationships made me a reasonable candidate for the job. Mike's faith in me provided a much-needed salve to my ego and gave me hope for the future. Recent experience proved that respect for your boss was critical to job satisfaction, and Mike certainly would have filled that need. I'd never thought about working at an architectural firm but could imagine the potential.

On the other hand, after thinking about Alecia and other volunteer opportunities that had brought me joy, I'd been considering shifting my career from local governments to the nonprofit world. I had a growing awareness that I especially loved creating opportunities for young people, so I told him I would think about it.

TURNING A VISION INTO REALITY

A few months after leaving the world of regional governance, I saw an article in the newspaper about the impending retirement of the executive director of the Boys & Girls Clubs of Oklahoma County, Doug Gibson. I asked to meet with him, and he was warm and encouraging as he shared his passion for the work and devotion to the organization. He told me how the Club had grown from serving kids in a small community building in the park to the recently completed much larger Clubhouse, but that he knew the need was still much greater than they could meet. He shared accolades about the current staff and the joy and importance of working with kids who so desperately needed a safe and inspiring place to be in their out-of-school time.

> In an anonymous survey of former Boys Club and Boys & Girls Club members, fifty-four percent of them said being part of the Club had saved their lives.

I decided to apply. It was my first job interview in over thirty years, and I was a bit intimidated by the process and the five distinguished gentlemen in business suits representing the Boys & Girls Clubs' leadership. I tried to convince them that my work with local governments and my volunteer experiences aligned with those of a nonprofit leader. I was hopeful, but that bubble of hopefulness burst when the board chair called to say they had chosen a candidate with several years of Boys & Girls Clubs' management experience. He was found to be a proven leader in the national organization and would be relocating to Oklahoma City from another state.

That evening, I shared a glass of wine with a friend and expressed my disappointment. I couldn't help but roll my eyes when he said, "You know, that guy could decide not to relocate. Maybe his wife refuses, the kids protest, he uses the offer as leverage for his current position…" I dismissed his words as futile encouragement from a buddy.

Later that week, lunch with my friend Mike from the architectural firm was lovely yet unsettling. I declined his generous offer, knowing that my decision defied logic. While I deeply appreciated his faith in me and encouragement to be on his team, for reasons that I didn't fully understand, I turned him down. I didn't have another option at the time, and even though the vision I had had faded in my mind, I had the sense that I was supposed to be waiting for something more.

Mike graciously accepted my decision and my recommendation to consider a former co-worker and friend for the position. I shared Nicolle's resume with Mike and enthusiastically described how she'd be perfect in the role. When she and I met for lunch a few days later and she talked about her shopping spree for clothes for her new job, I panicked. Why had I handed over that wonderful opportunity? Was I being courageous or just shortsighted?

I'd grown up in a Christian family and had always been grounded by a sense of faith. This was the first time, however, that I'd chosen an unknown and unforeseeable path over a perfectly good one based on where I believed God was leading me.

The call came two weeks later.

"Jane, this is Daria Butler, board chair of the Boys & Girls Clubs. The gentleman we hired as our next CEO decided not to move to Oklahoma for the position after all. Would you be willing to talk to us again?"

Elated, I met with Daria in his office the next day. On the way there, I mentally rehearsed potential lines of questioning, expecting a second round of interviews with the distinguished panel I'd previously met. When I arrived, however, Daria was the only one in the room. His first words stunned me, "When can you start as our president and CEO?"

I was surprised and briefly speechless yet buoyed by Daria's warmth and kind words of welcome. He offered the same compensation package they'd presented to the other candidate with Boys & Girls Clubs experience, which was generous and validating. I immediately accepted and embraced a new purpose in my life. I would now be living the mission of the Boys & Girls Clubs every hour of every day. My heart and spirit felt full of purpose and direction.

My first task was to better educate myself about the organization, its mission, and its impact. I thought about a BGCA study released just weeks before with remarkable statistics about *fifty-four percent* of former Club members who said that being part of the Boys & Girls

Club had *saved their lives*. What traumas had those adults faced as kids that made them feel they needed to be "saved"? And how could an after-school program really be that life-changing? I had not been fully aware of the magnitude of young people's dire need for mentors outside their families to help them reach their potential, nor of the ways this community organization was providing life-affirming relationships for at-risk children.

On my first day as president and CEO of the Boys & Girls Clubs of Oklahoma County, Dr. Joy Reed Belt, local gallery owner and philosopher extraordinaire, delivered a bouquet of beautiful flowers to my office with a handwritten note on her business card: "You will make a difference." I wondered how and if that would be true. I taped her note to the bottom of my computer monitor, where it remained as a constant reminder and message of hope.

CHAPTER 5
Pathways to Self-Acceptance

"Let today be the day you stand strong in the truth of your beauty. Journey through your day without attachment to the validation of others."

—Steve Maraboli

ANAMARIE

"I hate my body. I really don't want to go out. I can't find anything to wear, so why should I go? I can't even shop with my friends. I'll have to go to different stores for clothes or I'll be stuck looking at accessories again. I want to hang out with my friends, but I know I'm not the same as them. I know I don't fit in because I'm fat. I just wish I was somebody else!"

Those opening remarks in AnaMarie's competitive Youth of the Year speech captivated over four hundred people in attendance at the Club's annual gala. All-too-common issues of self-image and the desire to "measure up" to peers and social media expectations too frequently derail teenagers from recognizing and reaching their potential, and they had clearly threatened AnaMarie's well-being.

AnaMarie's emotional words struck a chord. The teen told the audience in the country club's grand ballroom how a ceremony welcoming ninth graders into high school had helped them make two important decisions: first, that AnaMarie, who later came out as non-binary and now uses they/he pronouns, was going to wear a dress, and second, that they would no longer wear clothes for anybody but themselves. AnaMarie said that the Boys & Girls Club had helped them create a new, more confident self and that they felt like they were starting high school as a new person.

AnaMarie's first memories of being part of the Club were as a first grader getting on the Club bus parked at their inner-city elementary school. AnaMarie stood in line next to the Under the Sea mural to catch a ride. Although basic childcare was the purpose of Club involvement in their younger days, it was the sense of well-being that kept AnaMarie participating through high school, even eventually becoming a staff member.

When AnaMarie joined as a child, the Club was in the small blue Kiwanis Club building in the park. "It was a little building with great possibilities," they told me years later. "Current Club members don't know how great they have it now in the new giant Clubhouse with amazing technology and other resources." But what mattered more than the brick-and-mortar building was the relationships. AnaMarie especially appreciated the encouragement and accountability from all the staff.

"On report card day, you could count on staff members at the front desk saying 'Let's see it! I need to see your report card!' as kids checked in. It made us feel cared for as well as accountable to someone we respected and loved." Fittingly, AnaMarie became a staff member years later and worked at the front desk. The former Club member quickly got to know each youngster by name and became that person who could encourage and hold them accountable.

AnaMarie's mom had finished only sixth grade in El Salvador before immigrating to America at age nineteen and later becoming a US citizen. AnaMarie's father was of Mexican descent, and their parents worked hard to provide for their loving family. They encouraged AnaMarie's education but knew any hope for college would depend on financial support. When we talked, AnaMarie credited the Boys & Girls Club with inspiring them to think about post-secondary education. College tours sponsored by the Club allowed them to visualize themselves in such an academic environment. AnaMarie said that those and other experiences created a confidence that otherwise would have been missing.

"If all you know is your family and the kids in your school, your view of the world and your opportunities can be very limited. The more people you see and know who are doing the things you want to do, the more you think you can do it. It makes it not so scary," AnaMarie said.

AnaMarie's path to becoming the state's Youth of the Year and competing at the regional BGCA level was a multi-year transformational process. With much encouragement from their staff mentor, AnaMarie first applied for the honor as a sophomore in high school. "It was like pulling teeth to get me to open up about my challenges and write my first couple of speeches. It hadn't been on my radar, but then it became my everything. I felt like I had something to say and that people were listening," AnaMarie said. Their competition speech the first year was basically a promotion for the Club, a description of the rooms and the programs housed in each. The second year, when they won the state competition, their speech was much more vulnerable and personal. That was when AnaMarie talked about struggling with body image and how being completely accepted for who they were at the Club gave them a dose of desperately needed confidence.

In a floor-length, flower-print taffeta dress, AnaMarie stepped out from behind the large wooden lectern at the country club with powerful closing remarks that touched every heart:

"And look at me," AnaMarie said, pausing for effect. "I'm standing here in front of all of you amazing people wearing a dress. And I think I look pretty good."

The crowd applauded wildly.

"The new me believes social media can take all their likes, dislikes, and comments and keep them. Because really, the only likes I'm going to need are going to come from me!" How validating and transformative it must have been for AnaMarie as they wrapped up these heartfelt comments to explosive applause and a standing ovation.

*AnaMarie and Jim Clark, CEO of BGCA,
at the Southwest Region Youth of the Year event*

When I caught up with AnaMarie years later at a coffee shop near their home, I was immediately struck by their poise and self-assuredness. With a sassy, asymmetrical, short and curly hairstyle, dangling earrings, and a multicolored mosaic sweater, they were quite charming. If I had not personally known AnaMarie years before, I could not have imaged them as a young teen who suffered mightily from poor self-esteem. Sitting in our corner booth, I was awestruck as they humbly shared their extensive list of accomplishments. Captivated by their successes, I wanted to know more about when, where, and how the transformation happened for AnaMarie to become a Magna Cum Laude college graduate and world-renowned speaker on mental health? I wondered what doors opened the potential of this child to create such a bright and meaningful future, despite the paralyzing insecurities of their youth?

And, there was another surprise… a sudden and unexpected role reversal! Our first meeting as two adults happened early in my discovery process about writing this book. When I shared my self-doubt and expressed concerns about whether anyone would be interested in what I had to write, they gave me the most encouraging response.

"Ms. Jane!" AnaMarie exclaimed with a quick flip of their hair and twist of their head. "*Where* is the Ms. Jane I knew who was CEO of the Boys & Girls Club and walked into any room with confidence and direction?" AnaMarie became *my* mentor that day and shared insightful and specific recommendations about what such a book might entail and how I might go about approaching its creation. In fact, when I learned that AnaMarie enjoyed doing research for their college classes, I hired them to do much of the research about the crises our country's youth are facing—which they did with aplomb. I told AnaMarie how touched I was by their interest and enthusiasm about my project, and they reminded me: "Even after you've graduated and moved on, people at the Boys & Girls Club are still family."

When AnaMarie started college, they capitalized on the many years of having strong mentors at the Boys & Girls Club by seeking further support. As a college freshman at the University of Central Oklahoma (UCO), they joined the Hispanic Success Initiative, an organization for first generation Hispanic students who were paired with a peer mentor and college professor. The organization helped freshmen learn about things like financial aid and resources on campus, which can be particularly daunting for first generation college students. The next year, AnaMarie became a mentor and continued in that role throughout the undergraduate college experience. AnaMarie said that the diversity of members and staff at the Boys & Girls Clubs had given them the awareness and background needed to relate with people from a wide range of cultures.

AnaMarie also worked as a Sexual Health Ambassador intern, student researcher, then coordinator at the UCO Women's BGLTQ+ Research Student Center. They have spoken to college classes, churches, and schools and have been honored to present research findings overseas on two different occasions. AnaMarie

> "Even after you've graduated from college and moved on, people at the Boys & Girls Club are still family."

traveled with a small group of students and faculty to make presentations at two conferences in India. Attendees valued their expertise and research related to the need for LGBTQ+ inclusivity and holistic care of queer patients, especially regarding training for future physicians.

When I met with AnaMarie again more recently, at a small coffee shop near the Club, I heard about a recent trip to Greece, where they had again traveled with a group of collegiate peers to share their research. This time, they had spoken on "Catholicism in the Latinx Community" at an international conference in Athens on religion and spirituality. Coming from a Catholic Latinx family, AnaMarie is interested in how tenants of Catholicism affect the mental health of their community of origin.

AnaMarie's college studies have highlighted passion for helping professions. They graduated Magna Cum Laude in interpersonal communication with a minor in psychology in 2022. At the time of this writing, AnaMarie is working on a master's degree in counseling psychology to become a licensed professional counselor, counseling students on campus, and interning at Edmond Family Counseling. The college graduate credits experiences at the Boys & Girls Clubs for "showing me the world of scholarships to afford my dreams."

While our times together did not have a "therapeutic" purpose, I know from personal experience that AnaMarie's gifts for understanding, acceptance, and encouragement can be life-affirming for anyone who is fortunate enough to engage them in conversation. I am certain they will be a wonderful counselor. AnaMarie has found meaning and purpose in helping others, including me, feel accepted for who they are.

LEO

"Whenever you open yourself up to a child, keep an open mind," Leo said. "Give no judgment or thought of what this person should be. They are about to tell you who they are, and that's okay. There's nothing better than walking into an environment where you just know someone is there to listen and understand."

Like AnaMarie, Leo also started attending the Boys & Girls Club when it was in the little community center building in the park and he was six years old. He told me years later that he was terrified at first, not realizing that it would soon become his home away from home and where he would later find the most acceptance as a young gay man.

Even at six years old, he was interested in the computers in the small computer lab, but he said most of them were broken and the line was always too long to wait for access. As an alternative, he enjoyed staying cool in the water park behind the Clubhouse, playing video games, and eating the Club's good snacks. He said his sister spent her time at their aunt's house nearby instead of being at the Club, but he enjoyed the camaraderie and activities at the Club.

When Leo began middle school, he joined every school organization possible, trying to establish his identity: cheerleading, dance, band, and the audio-visual team. Those activities kept him away from the Club for a couple of years, and during that time, the Boys & Girls Club tore down the small community center building and moved into the newly built larger Clubhouse. The new and expanded computer lab with working computers drew Leo back to the Club, but the impact of rejoining went far beyond learning computer skills.

"I was a chubby kid who liked boys," he said. "I started trying to figure myself out. The Boys & Girls Club helped me get out of my shell and make friends. It became a huge part of me in a lot of ways. My personality wouldn't be as open or friendly if I had not found that safe space at the Club. I was a weird kid who could do stuff but didn't. Starting in eighth grade, I went to the Club all the time, and began not caring about what other people thought of me. It helped me branch out to find the better part of me… and that was just the beginning," said Leo.

His staff mentor introduced Leo to performing on stage through a partnership with a local theater company. That multi-year experience provided an additional place for Leo to sing, dance, and make friends. He performed in the play *The Music Man* and enjoyed having his voice celebrated.

"LaRissa was a huge part of making this Leo," he said referring to the staff member who had mentored him. "She helped provide an environment where I could express myself without disapproval." He also developed close relationships with other staff in the computer lab and the kitchen. His beautiful voice opened many doors for him, including an opportunity to sing before a multi-state crowd of professionals and volunteers at a BGCA regional conference in Austin, Texas. He sang "I'm Here" from *The Color Purple* to a standing ovation. He later became a spokesperson on LGBTQ+ inclusion for BGCA, sharing his Club experiences in a nationally distributed video.

> "LaRissa was a huge part of making this Leo."

Leo competed in the Club's Youth of the Year program but said he never expected to win because he didn't enjoy writing speeches. "The way I talk to people is more of an informal and emotional connection," he said. "It's the way I feel in the moment, not a prepared speech." Going through that process required courage, however, and gave him a sense of accomplishment.

A special supporter of the Club and advocate of providing safe spaces for youth who identify as LGBTQ+ asked me once if it would be helpful to create a Boys & Girls Club specifically for queer kids. When I asked Leo what he thought about that idea, he said he understood the thinking behind that concept: a safe space to meet others who understood and to not have to worry about judgment or dirty glances. On the other hand, he said that a separate club might make members feel even more ostracized, and that it is more important to normalize their situation. Leo reminded me that all are welcome at the Boys & Girls Club. He has had multiple examples of being bullied at school, but never at the Club.

In addition to finding a safe space, Leo also landed several job opportunities through his involvement at the Club. He started working as a junior staff member in the Club kitchen at age thirteen. He enjoyed the relationship with the ladies who managed the important role of feeding Club kids their after-school snacks and breakfast and lunch during school breaks. Providing nutritious meals is an important part of realizing the Boys & Girls Club's healthy lifestyles vision.

He later worked with a staff member who was trained to be a job coach through BGCA's workforce development program. She helped Leo and several others apply for and succeed at part-time positions with Old Navy clothing stores. The store where Leo worked was within walking distance from the Club.

Leo told me that one challenge for young men who are gay is building friendships with straight guys, because straight boys are often suspicious that a gay boy might want a romantic relationship. "There's an edge to it," he said, and that can be hurtful. He found his best "straight-guy-friend" at the Club, and they have remained close even after high school graduation.

After graduation and more than six years working in the kitchen at the Club, Leo felt stagnant and that it was time to get out of his comfort zone. He is now working at a popular restaurant and aspires to become an event planner. I was able to connect him with a local restaurant entrepreneur who gave him very sage advice and encouragement. Leo dreams of establishing working relationships with people to help create welcoming and joyful ways to celebrate special occasions in their lives. I have no doubt that his will be a legacy of inclusion, joy, and love.

CHAPTER 6
For Such a Time as This

"To inspire and enable all youth, especially those who need us most, to reach their full potential as responsible, productive, and caring citizens."

—Boys & Girls Clubs of America (BGCA)
Mission Statement

Even my best crock-pot chili couldn't warm the room. As I searched the disinterested faces of the dedicated Boys & Girls Club staff I was supposed to lead, the problem was clear: they didn't want me. The tight team of full-time staff had worked together for several years and with considerable autonomy. One member of the group had also applied for the CEO position for which I'd just been hired, creating natural resistance to an outsider coming in.

I brought homemade chili and appetizing fixings to our first Monday staff meeting in an effort to build comradery. My face was swollen with an excruciating abscessed tooth making my speech slow and slurred, yet the blank stares around the table, lack of conversation, and disinterest in my homemade lunch offerings stung even more.

Despite the rough start, our administrative offices were in the Clubhouse, and the life and laughter of children coming in after school immediately boosted my spirits. From the youngest kindergartners to aspiring high school seniors, there was a family atmosphere of love and acceptance. Right away, it was obvious to me what a tremendous difference the Club was making in these children's and teenagers' lives. At the time, we served about four hundred youth after school and during school breaks. Coming there meant they had a safe place to be with nourishing snacks, help with homework, caring adult mentors, a variety of friends, and opportunities for recreation and multiple extra-curricular activities. Without the Club, most of them would have been home alone in neighborhoods fraught with gangs, drugs, and violence. Statistics show the most dangerous part of the day for most kids is during after-school hours before parents or guardians return from work. Even when not in physical danger, they are most vulnerable to negative influences.

Will Jawando, author of *My Seven Black Fathers*, writes that one of the powerful indicators of a child's future comes from what he or she does each day between 3:00 and 6:00 p.m. Are they "decision" kids or "destination" kids? Decision kids are children who must decide for themselves what they'll be doing during those hours. Destination kids have locked in activities or places to go. Consistent with the response to the national survey of Boys & Girls Club alums, Jawando writes that distinction literally can make the difference between life and death.

Boys & Girls Clubs members have a "locked in destination."

Aware of the kind of impact the Club experience could potentially have on our community's disadvantaged youth filled me with angst. The initial lukewarm staff reception in contrast to the critical importance of the work weighed heavily on me, and self-doubt took hold.

> Between the hours of 3:00 and 6:00 p.m. are they destination kids or decision kids? That can make the difference between life and death.

While I expected it to take time, it was a rougher start than I imagined. And there was so much at stake! Was I up to the challenge? These children and staff were depending on me. Did I have the intellect, experience, and resources to serve them well? Was I the right person to gather the best team and lead? Was trust in God enough? My confidence was shaken.

Then it happened! Standing in the Clubhouse lobby, I saw in real life the scene that had flashed as a vision in my mind months before: children of various ages and ethnicities running, jumping, laughing, and shouting with joy!

It was the very scene I had envisioned on that terrible day when I was dismissed from a thirty-year career! Yet this time, it was unfolding in real life in the lobby of a Boys & Girls Club. This time, I felt the brisk January wind blasting through the double glass doors as the kids raced into the building. I heard their chatter and shrieks of joy. I saw their faces light up as they connected with their favorite staff member at the front desk. I smelled the scent of cookies baking in the Clubhouse kitchen and watched as the kids lined up to take their turns for snacks. I marveled at their differences and similarities and felt such gratitude that I could share this moment with them.

That vision hadn't crossed my mind in months. Watching it come to life filled me with joy, amazement, and affirmation. A special supporter of the Club asked me later that week how I had ended up in this position, and I could humbly answer that I believed God had led me there. What a glorious gift it was to know that at least for that moment of time, I was where He intended for me to be—abscessed tooth and all. Now, if only He could help me bring the team together to realize our collective potential.

Additional "signs and wonders" began to appear and gave me courage, strength, and direction in my new role. In his book *When God Winks at You*, Squire Rushnell describes how God speaks to people through the power of coincidence, which he calls "godwinks." He believes they are personal messages of reassurance that no matter how uncertain your life seems at a certain point in time, He will help move you toward certainty.

Whether you call them godwinks, purposeful accidents, miracles, or just good karma, I had several such assurances following the real-life enactment of the vision in the Clubhouse lobby. Enter the Grader Guy, the Zumba Girl, the Lectern, the Shelter in the Storm, and the BGCA angel who all reminded me of God's faithfulness.

THE GRADER GUY

After that first week on the job, Oklahoma City experienced a rare occurrence: a snowstorm with rooftop-high drifts making it impossible to get to the front door of the Club. Oklahoma is not known for or well prepared for such blizzards. With little to no warning, families were home without food or heat. Some Club members' parents had jobs that required them to go to work. Their kids needed to be with us where they'd be warm, fed, and cared for.

While the entire city shut down the Monday after the storm, I sat at home, desperately seeking the means to re-open the Club the following day. Our board chair had identified someone who might clear the parking lot, but he called at 3:00 that afternoon to say it was no longer an option. I sat in my favorite reading chair in my bedroom and, out of exasperation, exclaimed, "What are we going to do, God?" I felt responsible, discouraged, and powerless. For some irrational reason, I thought that putting on my snow boots and walking out to our mailbox might clear my head. That was when I got the second big wink.

My residential street is only one block long with a dead end. As I trudged through the snow to our mailbox by the curb, a guy in a truck with a giant grader affixed to the front was driving toward our house. Years later, I can still picture him clearing off snow as he drove down my street and remember thinking, "Really, God? You sent me a grader guy with a snow plow?"

After frantically waving for him to stop, I explained my dilemma. Wanting to make it safe for families who depended on us, he and his buddies drove the twenty miles to the Club that night. Street lights in the park made it possible for them to see and remove the snow and ice. They not only made the parking lot passable but completely cleared the wide sidewalk leading up to the front door. Their generosity brought new meaning to the Biblical promise that God will make clear our paths. Indeed, He did.

THE ZUMBA GIRL

When summer came and kids were out of school, the number of our Club members ballooned. Once waiting lists got too long, all staff could do was tell parents to try again during next season's open enrollment. (We made exceptions for kids in the foster care system.) That scorching hot summer, program staff were forced to lock the doors of the Club once we reached fire code occupancy limits—usually before noon. Turning kids away in the heat of the day was heart-wrenching, knowing that they likely had no other safe, cool place to be with food to eat or adult supervision.

It was clearly time to expand.

Given the need to strengthen our financial footing to grow, the role of our business manager required upgrading. The woman who had been working there for several years was already completely overwhelmed by the tasks at hand. She often was found watching movies on her computer to escape the paperwork piles on her desk. Utility notices threatening to cut off electricity, natural gas, phones, and internet services piled up. Late fees were mounting. It was virtually impossible to track financial pledges and donations. The thought of turning kids away because the water or lights had been shut off was intolerable. It became critical to bring in a person with more financial expertise to serve as the business manager, yet there couldn't be a gap between the overwhelmed employee and a new hire.

BGCA requires local organizations to follow strict guidelines of safety, evidence-based programing, and fiscal accountability. The national organization maintains the highest GuideStar Platinum Seal of Transparency and is ranked on the Chronicle of Philanthropy's list of "America's Favorite Charities." As a leader, having integrity with local donors was of import as well. The pressure of maintaining that financial standard of excellence weighed heavily on me.

Perplexed, I went to my Saturday morning Zumba class at a local YMCA. It was a very popular class, so participants arrived early to claim their spot on the gym floor several minutes before starting time. As I sat cross-legged on the floor, I couldn't help but overhear a conversation between two young women in front of me. They talked about the good time they'd had the night before, having cocktails on the roof of a local restaurant. They said it was especially enjoyable because they both felt like the previous week had been a disaster. Adrienne Burden was one of the young women, and she expressed frustration with her current job. While her accounting skills and experience seemed to be appreciated, the negatives outweighed the positives.

"I have decided that I just need to find a good and honest place to go to work," she said.

"Excuse me," I interrupted. "I couldn't help overhearing your conversation. I know it's a longshot, but I may have what you want. And you may have what I desperately need."

Adrienne met me at the Club later that afternoon. After checking references, I found her to have the perfect skill set, competence, and passion to take our organization's financial acumen to the next level. Over the next several months, she established a solid fiscal footing on which we could build the future of the organization. Her enthusiasm and expertise also helped bring the team together.

And to make a tough situation even better, after the hard conversation with the person for whom the job had become overwhelming, she told me that the change was the best outcome for her, too. She had been miserable but loved the kids and staff at the Club—and similar to my previous feelings at ACOG, she hadn't known how to leave.

THE LECTERN

Dell Computers invested hundreds of thousands of dollars in building a state-of-the-art computer lab at the Boys & Girls Club in 2011. Instead of sauntering into a makeshift computer lab with a handful of obsolete, dysfunctional computers, Club members now impatiently waited their turn to enter a functional, high-tech computer center that would be the envy of any organization.

On their own time (including an overnight stay by a network-server expert), Dell volunteers installed twenty-five new computer stations housed in sleek black desks, with a master station for the staff leader and a giant drop-down wall screen for instructional purposes. The advanced computer lab created an environment for completing high-tech classroom assignments and exploring future career opportunities.

Few Club members have up-to-date technology or high-speed internet access at home. Staff support and experience in the lab leveled the digital playing field for our under-resourced Club members making time in the Club's new Dell lab both motivational and inspirational. Plans were in the works for leaders from Dell's corporate offices in Texas to come to town for a big press conference publicizing their tremendous gift. They were also to be recognized at the Boys & Girls Clubs' Corporate Champion of Youth event the following night.

The computer giant's executives had high expectations for the logistics of the press conference at the Club. Their run of show expectations included a draped background display and a professional lectern from which to speak. Pipe-and-drape was easy to rent, but the Club didn't own a lectern, and they were expensive and unbudgeted. When the stand offered by another local nonprofit a few days before the event turned out to be a substandard flimsy metal music stand, once again, I exclaimed out loud in exasperation, "What are we going to do?"

Just as I exited the room where we were staging the press conference, a scruffy, unkept gentleman walked in the lobby doors and asked for the director. I reluctantly introduced myself, and Brent expressed his desperation. He needed to find a community service job right away to "pay his dues" for a DUI he had received a few weeks earlier. He wanted to go out of state, and the judge required him to complete and document his community service before leaving town.

He was familiar with our building because he had previously helped wire the Clubhouse for internet. Still reeling about our lectern dilemma, I asked him if he had any carpentry experience. He said, "A little," and hesitantly agreed to build a wooden lectern quickly for the Dell press conference. Brent did not just build an ordinary lectern but crafted a beautiful four-foot-high and two-foot-wide solid oak masterpiece with nice trim, a lip, and shelf to hold the speaker's remarks. It provided a professional anchor for the stage and gave us confidence that we would represent Dell and the Club well.

Even after Brent had completed his community service requirements, he continued volunteering at the Club nearly every day, doing handyman projects as needed. With four hundred kids in the building, they were always needed. Being at the Club with our staff and kids, and providing a service for others, bolstered his self-esteem and sense of purpose. It put him on the path for more meaningful employment. One day, he walked in the front doors of the Club clean-shaven and wearing a suit and tie to tell us he had a new job and would need to switch his volunteer time to evenings or weekends instead of weekdays.

I knew then that a carpenter from Biblical times had opened the door for the Boys & Girls Clubs to impact Brent's life as well.

SHELTER IN THE STORM

A young man named Jon Thompson and his bride had recently moved to town from Canada. While his wife was born in the US, he was a native Canadian and did not yet have his government green card, making him ineligible for paid employment. They had both been involved in mission work, and he was interested in learning more about nonprofit organizations. He asked if he could volunteer in the administrative offices. He wanted to work eight hours a day, Monday through Friday, with no pay: a true blessing for an organization struggling to make ends meet.

Organizational finances were tight, and his offer seemed almost too good to be true. We invited him to tour the Club to give us a chance to get to know him and, honestly, to determine if he was for real. He had a quiet, polite manner, and we were impressed with his stated goals.

And then the rains came! Jon started on a Monday just hours before major thunderstorm and massive dirt work in the city park caused the most significant flooding the Club had ever experienced. My heart dropped when the youth development staff leader called me after he opened the Club doors at 6:30 the next morning. "Ms. Jane, there is water above my ankles throughout the building!"

Organization founders built the Clubhouse in a beloved, expansive park in the heart of the city. Cities often create parks on low-lying lands, including flood plains. While engineers and architects considered the elevations when they designed the thirty-five-thousand-square-foot building, in hindsight, it was more vulnerable to flooding than expected, and the significant upgrades the city was making in the park were more than our building could handle.

Nearly the entire Clubhouse had flooded overnight, and water and debris were continuing to seep through the walls. We were faced with a major disaster recovery effort.

Mild-mannered Jon immediately transformed into a volunteer superhero, pulling up and dumping squares of completely soaked and very heavy carpet into grocery carts to be wheeled out to the dumpster. He set an amazing example of great personal sacrifice with no monetary reward.

We were forced to hire disaster mitigation professionals and close the Club for a few days for carpet to be tossed, holes in the walls to be drilled to prevent mold, and furniture and equipment to be replaced. The disruption to our kids and families would have lasted weeks longer without the dedication of several staff members and one bionic volunteer.

Jon worked day after day, week after week, for over four months without complaint and for no compensation, before he finally got his green card and joined the team as a paid employee. We both cried with joy when that day came.

ROBIN, A BGCA ANGEL

Although I was new to this role as a nonprofit leader, executives of Boys & Girls Club organizations never start from scratch or alone. An army of mission-driven soldiers empowers them to be successful in their efforts to create life-changing opportunities for the youth in their communities. My BGCA angel was Robin Schmidt. Within my first week on the job, she was sitting by my side, connecting me to a national cadre of professionals whose shared purpose was to help young people, especially those with limited resources, reach their potential and become caring citizens.

BGCA had been around for over 160 years and had amassed hundreds of evidenced-based best practices in working with children and teens. To carry forward the stellar tradition of Boys & Girls Clubs, organizations were required to meet numerous rigorous standards to ensure that youth in their care experience opportunities that enrich their lives.

One of those standards was the requirement that new executives attend a week-long training within their first ninety days on the job. During my orientation, Robin and many of her peers poured into me not only the mechanics of running a successful nonprofit organization, but perhaps more importantly, the WHY! In retrospect, I believe that God used a closed door in my earlier career to catapult me into finding my ultimate career purpose living the WHY of the Boys & Girls Clubs.

EXPLOSIVE EXPANSION WITH SCHOOL PARTNERSHIPS

When I began as CEO in January 2011, I realized it was taking time for staff members' minds to imagine the expansiveness of possibilities with the additional space of the new thirty-five-thousand-square-foot Clubhouse. I felt that it was an important part of my job to fill every inch with enriching programs and opportunities. Over time, we were able to bring in more community partners to make the enlarged space come to life with dance, art, robotics, computers, leadership programs, reading, a variety of sports teams, and the like. Club experiences increased tenfold. The expanded Clubhouse also provided space to recruit and welcome a variety of community volunteers who broadened the influence and outreach available for our members.

Once we felt confident in our efforts to serve youth most effectively at our Memorial Park Club, we began investigating other areas of the community where there were critical needs. In that discovery process, we learned that many Boys & Girls Clubs around the country gather in school buildings. Offering out-of-school-time services within school walls provides an efficient way to serve more youth without additional building and transportation costs.

We invited potential partners from area schools to discuss the possibility of collaborating to serve their students with a Club experience. A giant map of the region provided important points of reference for consideration. The map showed zip codes of the greatest number of families living in poverty and where their children went to school.

After reviewing the needs and interest from educators, the board directed its attention to schools in the southern part of Oklahoma City, where the urgency for after-school programs for youth seemed to be most critical. Two generous financial opportunities to support kids in that area of town surfaced nearly simultaneously: Cesar

Chavez Elementary in the Oklahoma City Public School District (funded through the Ken and Gae Rees Family Fund at Oklahoma City Community Foundation) and Santa Fe South Elementary, part of Santa Fe South Charter Schools (funded with 21st Century federal and state dollars).

The two south Oklahoma City school-site Clubs started within a couple of months of each other. Santa Fe South Club began at the charter school in the fall of 2013, and the Cesar Chavez Club at the traditional public school in January 2014. They created fruitful opportunities for building solid partnerships with school districts to serve more kids, more often, with greater impact. Establishing the framework for future partnerships with schools quadrupled the number of youth the Boys & Girls Clubs of Oklahoma County was able to serve in a short period of time.

Area local government officials also took notice of the difference the Boys & Girls Clubs were making for families in their communities. A city councilperson and city manager from Midwest City approached the Oklahoma County organization about providing services for kids in their community. We jumped at the chance to expand our reach to another acute area of need within the county, opening our first Midwest City Club in 2015. Success in that program quickly led to a new partnership with the Mid-Del School District to start a second Midwest City Club in 2019.

The same year, the City of Oklahoma City chose the Boys & Girls Clubs of Oklahoma County to start programs at Adelaide Lee Elementary and Capitol Hill Middle School. Both schools are in neighborhoods that were part of the City's Strong Neighborhood Initiative program to provide multifaceted services for families in those struggling neighborhoods.

Another milestone that year was completion of a 6,200-square-foot expansion to our original Memorial Park Clubhouse to serve more teens. With their own entrance to the Club, enhanced technology, and support for high school graduation and beyond, the new Teen Center addition opened a world of opportunity for older Club members.

As the Boys & Girls Clubs of Oklahoma County organization reached its quarter-of-a-century milestone in 2020, it celebrated its expansion from one small Club site first serving fifty youth to six locations throughout the county serving over four thousand children and teens.

After my retirement in May 2020, during the height of the COVID pandemic, Teena and Club leadership stepped up to serve even more youth with expanded hours in the areas of greatest need. The team developed a two-year COVID-19 Recovery Plan for Kids. They increased efforts in academic enrichment and tutoring and added a partnership with another local nonprofit to provide a mental health professional at each Club site. They were able to garner more support from state and federal governments as a response to the impact of the pandemic on these most vulnerable children, which resulted in increased public support for Clubs throughout the entire state.

They also added focus to evidence-based programs in resiliency and coping skills and provided extensive training for staff on trauma-informed practices, conscious discipline, the science of hope, and more.

At the time of this writing, in 2024, there are eighteen Club locations serving over sixteen thousand children and teens throughout the Central Oklahoma area. Plans for four new Youth Centers sponsored by Oklahoma City's MAPS4 initiative are underway, further expanding the organization's reach and promising hope for thousands more youth throughout the community.

CHAPTER 7
Rising Resilience

"On the other side of a storm is the strength that comes from having navigated through it. Raise your sail and begin."

—Gregory S. Williams

VERONICA

Veronica started going to the Boys & Girls Club when she was six years old while her mom worked eighty-hour weeks to launch a new nonprofit for recovering alcoholics. As a recovering alcoholic herself, Veronica's mom was dedicated to helping others in the community struggling with addiction. Veronica was a lively little girl with light-brown hair and sparkling green eyes, who loved the activities at the Club and quickly developed close relationships with the staff and fellow Club members.

When she became a teenager, however, her mom and stepdad divorced, and she and her mom went to live with Veronica's older sister, brother-in-law, and niece. Their house was farther away from the Boys & Girls Club, and she was no longer able to attend. Even when her mom and sister were home and the house was full, Veronica said she felt alone and empty. There was little time for any of the adults in her life to pay attention to her needs.

"I felt isolated, and my depression was at an all-time high. My mom was so overworked that the dominant impression I had of her was when she was angry or yelling at me. My big sister was always in her room with the door closed," Veronica told me, years later.

"When I was fourteen, I planned to hang myself," explained Veronica. "I went to my best friend's house to say goodbye, and my friend's mom overheard our conversation. She alerted my mom to the depths of my depression and plans to end my life, and supports were put in place to keep me alive."

> "I put on a pleasant face at school, but when I got to the Club, I got to be my real self. Every day, my staff mentor asked me how I was doing and to list five positive things I could say about myself."

Fortunately, after Veronica's plans to end her life came to light, her mom made the commitment to make sure she could return to the Club. When I first started working there, I had not yet met Veronica, but my interest in her story came alive when I met her mom at a parent meeting. I was inspired by her mom's expression of deep gratitude for the Club's support during her daughter and their family's most trying time. Things had gotten more on track by the time I met them, and I wanted to know more about their struggles and how they had overcome them.

"The caring adults at the Boys & Girls Club helped me come back to thinking life was worth living," Veronica told me. "I put on a pleasant face at school and pretended to be happy, but when I got to the Club, I got to be my real self. Every day, my staff mentor asked me how I was doing and to list five positive things I could say about myself."

Surrounded by caring adults, homework help, and interesting activities, Veronica re-engaged and became a leader in various Club activities and programs. She loved honing her basketball skills and helping younger Club members. By the time I met her, she was a leader. She tutored others, organized fun games in the gym, and even found her way into the administrative offices, where she helped create order for those of us working behind the scenes. Instead of making me feel ashamed for the unorganized stacks of papers in my office, she carefully sorted and filed them on my behalf.

Veronica's newfound energy, confidence, and demonstrated leadership led staff to encourage her to apply to be the Club's Youth of the Year. She felt proud to be named Oklahoma County's Club Youth of the Year as an eighth grader, much younger than the typical honoree who was usually a high school junior or senior.

Not everyone was as happy about her success initially, however. Publicly sharing her story and her personal hurts during the process was a shock to her family members. Her mom was out of town at the time and unable to attend the dinner celebration where her daughter gave her speech. Veronica had never lived with her biological father, but he had been involved in her life, so he attended the event. She said he was upset with her afterwards for not making it clear that he wasn't to blame for her problems. When her mother and sister heard about her remarks, they were shocked that she had felt so alone and that she was willing to share her private feelings with hundreds of dinner attendees, but not with her own family.

When we got together in a local salad shop years later, Veronica told me that although it had created tension at the time, sharing her story as part of the Youth of the Year process had initiated deeper family communication. It had helped them became more familiar with each other's challenges and fears, and resulted in more understanding, forgiveness, and redemption. It provided a needed release of pent-up feelings and a platform for the family to talk through painful issues.

"I had been everybody's glue, and it felt good to share my feelings out loud," she said.

Her sister apologized for the previous lack of attention. She later told Veronica that the door to their room was usually closed because her now ex-husband was physically and emotionally abusive. She had been trying to hide the situation from the rest of the family. Her mom was struggling with her own depression and anxiety while working to build a nonprofit organization to help others.

After Veronica's mom discovered her plans to end her life, she feared her daughter would become an alcoholic or drug addict and refused to get her help that might have involved medication. Her mom reminded her daily, "You know your mom and dad are addicts, so you will probably be one too."

Veronica resented being put under that constant cloud of fear.

"If everyone would share what each other is dealing with, our world would be more understanding and a better place," she told me. "I am so glad our society is talking more about mental health and that schools are more focused on students' emotional well-being. I love that we now tell people, 'It is okay to not be okay.'"

"My generation is over hiding our issues with mental illness and substance abuse, and the problems our families have had. We are telling our stories and listening to each other. And we are not just listening, but acting upon what we have learned."

Sadly, Veronica has had more practice than most twenty-four-year-olds in learning to accept that it is okay to not be okay. While a freshman in college, she fell in love with a young man whose life ended tragically in an automobile accident. A specific cause was never identified, but Matthew had suffered from seizures in the past, so there was speculation that a seizure had caused him to cross the median and crash head-on into a truck. Veronica called me in tears, and a few days later, I attended the memorial service she and his mom held at a local mega church, with inspirational music and multiple testimonials about what a great young man he was. She had been living with his single mom and felt obligated to continue to stay with her for several months to help her through her grief while she grieved herself.

We periodically got together for a meal or a snack during Veronica's dark days. Unlike before, however, she knew she had the strength and support to continue through the pain. I remember sitting across from her on a Sunday afternoon at a local barbeque restaurant, watching her tears of despair, but thankful for her quick reassurance that this time she had no plans to end her life.

Veronica worked as many hours as she could at a local restaurant and applied for scholarship assistance to pay for her bachelor's degree at the University of Central Oklahoma. She is now in graduate school working toward a master's degree in addiction counseling with hopes to become a licensed alcohol and drug counselor. Working for the nonprofit her mom founded, Oklahoma Citizens Advocate for Recovery Transformation Association (OCARTA), Veronica serves as director of operations, accounts payable and family care coordinator. Besides watching the finances of the organization, she is also part of a We Care program through the University of Oklahoma Stars Clinic. She and others identify pregnant women living on the streets who are interested in coming off harmful substances. The program helps the expectant mothers create a drug- and alcohol-free care plan for after their babies arrive. They meet weekly while the women are pregnant and maintain monthly visits after the baby is born.

"Because the love and compassion shown to me at the Boys & Girls Club gave me love and compassion for youth, I also regularly volunteer on weekends and evenings with OCARTA's youth programs," she told me. "We offer support groups and resources for teens who have substance abuse problems in their families."

Clearly, Veronica understands the challenges faced by young people and uses her experience and wisdom to guide them. In fact, when I got a call from another former Club kid who was struggling, Veronica quickly came to our aide with multiple suggestions about resources for a positive path forward.

Veronica has started a family of her own and wants her baby girl to always feel loved and supported as she grows through both happy and difficult seasons of her life. When I attended her sweet daughter's "Holy Cow I'm One" birthday party, I was impressed with the festive pink and cow balloons, pinatas, and decorations, but most inspired by and grateful for her daughter's twinkling blue eyes, three-toothed smile, and hands wildly clapping to the music and waving to the crowd of partygoers. Veronica's compassion, intellect, and drive are and will continue to be models for resilience, leaving a legacy for overcoming adversity, addiction, and despair. She continues to invest in a more hopeful world.

CHAPTER 8
Purpose Bigger than a Paycheck

"I don't know what your destiny will be, but one thing I know: the only ones among you who will be really happy are those who have sought and found how to serve."

—Albert Schweitzer

Although the reception I got from Club staff my first week on the job was less than enthusiastic, it didn't take me long to see how members of the team were committed to helping all kids who came through those blue doors reach their potential. As a relatively new organization, I knew how important it was to identify the staff leaders who could emerge as mentors for each other as well as the kids they served. Over time, we developed a cohesive team that would set the stage for continued growth, both in size and in impact. Boys & Girls Clubs all around the country hire compassionate staff who each have their own stories that create the secret sauce of their organizations. During the discovery process for this book, I revisited a few members of our team whose transformative power I was privileged to experience. I wanted to learn more about what brought them to this work and what lessons they had to share.

LARISSA CONN

"I decided I couldn't watch another kid give up because I couldn't find a way to help," said LaRissa about the heartbreaking experience that transformed her life and career direction. After college graduation, she was working for a church that bused middle school and high school kids from neighboring communities to an after-school program in an old converted theater. She said most of the kids came from small rural towns with predominately white residents. The exceptions were the kids from "the flats," where most of the impoverished Black and Hispanic families lived. While LaRissa connected closely with those kids, some of the church leadership questioned their involvement.

One night, a fight broke out during the program, and although they were not the instigators, the kids from the flats were blamed. Church leadership decided that they could no longer afford to bus kids to the program from as far away as the flats and gave LaRissa the untenable task of sharing the bad news on their fifteen-minute bus ride back home. That experience turned out to be a pivotal moment in her life, and years later, the lessons learned brought her to the Boys & Girls Clubs.

On that heart-shattering bus ride, Charles, the outwardly toughest kid in the group, asked to be dropped off last. As soon as the next-to-last person got off, his tough-guy demeanor melted away, replaced by unstoppable tears.

"You can't do this!" he pleaded. "I've been trying to get out of this town for the longest time. You can't stop! I'll do anything you want. Please don't just leave me."

LaRissa had grown up thinking an employee should just comply with whatever their employer asked them to do, so she explained that although she was sorry, she couldn't change the situation. She said Charles's exterior immediately went back to its stoic tough-guy self.

"The bricks went back up. I watched him completely shut down when we didn't show up for him." Two weeks later, police arrested Charles on a weapons charge.

LaRissa credits that middle school kid from the flats and his unanswered cries for help for teaching her that she couldn't put herself in that position again.

> "The bricks went back up. I watched him completely shut down when we didn't show up for him."

She and her sister still talk about the mission trip they took with their church to Panama City Beach when she was a teenager. It was on that trip that LaRissa discovered her gift for relating to kids. She believed there was a reason she felt so at home in those situations.

LaRissa had grown up singing in church and working with youth. She thought that becoming a classroom teacher or youth minister were the only two career paths for her success and happiness. Being an extraordinary staff person at the Boys & Girls Club was never on her radar or in her imagination. She now emphatically tells others, "You don't have to rely on a certain degree for your mission. Your mission is within you. I'm so thankful that I have found my mission at home at the Boys & Girls Club."

While initially following the schoolteacher path, LaRissa worked toward a degree in education at college until she realized "it didn't fit." During her sophomore year, a professor gave the students an assignment to create a portfolio for classroom instruction.

"I got really creative with it, and it was great," she said with a smile.

However, her professor had a different opinion. "Start over. This is not professional," he barked. That experience made her realize that being a teacher in a standard education setting would likely be too stifling for her creative spirit, and she immediately changed her major to interpersonal communications, with a minor in psychology. LaRissa took that direction because it enabled her to carry over her course credits in education and still graduate on time. More importantly, however, she soon realized that she had landed in the right place as she began soaking up her learning.

While in college, LaRissa enjoyed working in campus ministry. Several churches recruited her to serve as a youth leader after graduation, which seemed like a logical next step. And it was, until… she hit the major personal roadblock. Disillusioned and without a clear sense of direction after the situation with the abandoned church program and upset teen, she stepped away from youth development and waited tables for a few years until a nonprofit opportunity came up to work with youth in a substance abuse prevention program.

LaRissa started hitting her stride, learning from her past experiences and remembering the good feelings that came from service to others, particularly kids. It was the first time that she had worked with youth who didn't automatically want to listen to her, though. In her church group work, she had always introduced herself on stage, providing music and lessons, and was able to gain credibility and trust with those kids before trying to have one-on-one conversations. In the first week working at the middle school, the girls she tried to talk to "legit ignored me," she told me. "I learned from that experience that kids don't initially trust and won't automatically listen. It's important to prove yourself first to build their trust."

LaRissa resigned from A Chance to Change when the organization didn't have the funds to continue to pay teachers for their planning periods. By quitting, she would free up funds for others, and she didn't want to relive an experience where funding caused abandonment of kids.

She went back to waiting tables, but one day, a close friend confronted her. "LaRissa! Kids are waiting for you! What are you afraid of? What is holding you back?" LaRissa told me later that everyone needs a friend like that who will step on your toes and to tell you what you need to hear.

Little did she know when she applied for a part-time summer job at the Boys & Girls Club, the vast number of lives she would impact and the organizational leader and mentor she would become. Her musical and creative talents immediately drew kids to her, but above all, her unique and powerful ways of making them feel seen and heard made her a favorite. She was extraordinarily gifted at seeing a child's heart and connecting their innermost desires and talents with other people and activities at the Club to spark their potential.

She also worked well with fellow staff members, organizational leadership, and volunteers, to the point that Club administrative staff became determined to fund her involvement as a full-time employee. LaRissa became our first full-time volunteer coordinator and worked tirelessly to bring people from the community into the Club to provide attention and opportunities for its members. She built lasting relationships with many individuals and organizations and helped elevate community awareness of the magical things that were happening beyond our blue doors.

"All kids need someone who thinks they are the best, and one of my favorite things is to watch the multi-day afterglow after a group of volunteers leave," she said. LaRissa explained that most of the kids who come to

Purpose Bigger than a Paycheck

Boys & Girls Clubs don't have networks of extended families, friends, and outside groups of people who can show them that they matter.

LaRissa worked hard to bring in community arts organizations to enrich Club members' experiences and create interest in things to which they otherwise would have very little access. Local theater and ballet companies, choral groups, and visual artists became regular participants in building Club members' appreciation for the arts—and most importantly, offered opportunities to participate.

She delighted in watching Club kids find their own voices and stand up for causes they believed in. She has mentored junior staff members, many of whom grew up in the Club as kids, and finds special joy in their accomplishments.

As the COVID pandemic began, it became apparent that the organization needed a very special leader to manage activities at the Club, and management chose LaRissa as the Memorial Park Club unit director. Her ability to be flexible and adjust and readjust with daily changes of school closings and illnesses of staff and kids provided amazing leadership. Her unrivaled compassion provided the glue that kept it all together.

She later led the charge to encourage the CEO who followed me to find resources to take several key staff members to a national BGCA Conference, citing in the memo the difference attending such a conference with me had made to her earlier in her career.

"We traveled to St. Louis, and my eyes were opened to just how much bigger than myself this movement of Boys & Girls Club actually is. I was able to meet the vice president of our region and hear how they were all strategizing to grow both in quantity and quality, listen to how these amazing leaders planned and navigated issues, and picture myself in similar circumstances someday. But more importantly, I got the chance to see how sweeping this movement is for so many others... Clubs dealing with all of the same issues we were dealing with. I got to sit in trainings with board members from all over the Southwest Region and gain a fuller understanding of all the sacrifices they make, both personally and professionally, to have a seat on their boards and use their voices in rooms where Club staff were not frequenting," she wrote.

"I know that I wouldn't be where or who I am today without the Club choosing to invest in me as a potential leader." LaRissa is building legacies of leadership, creativity, and compassion every day.

A.Jaye Johnson, Jane Sutter, and LaRissa Conn

A.JAYE JOHNSON

"I *had* to get back to those kids; I *needed* them," said A.Jaye, describing his arduous and multi-month climb back to health following a series of devastating strokes.

Years earlier as a young man, A.Jaye had accidently fallen into his calling as a youth development professional. Working at a YMCA while in college in Weatherford, Oklahoma, A.Jaye noticed three little boys who came with their babysitter while she exercised in the fitness center. He engaged them while he did maintenance jobs around the Y, and they quickly became his best helpers, following him everywhere.

Management noticed how the boys were hanging on A.Jaye's every move and asked him if he would help with the next event they called "No School Fun Day" for kids, then Friday Family Skate Nights (the gymnasium converted to a roller-skating rink). This led to putting him temporarily in charge of the Y one summer, when all the management employees were on vacation at the same time.

He loved working with those kids, but when his dad became critically ill, he became weary of the long drive back and forth and decided to move back to Oklahoma City (his hometown) to be closer to his family. Saying goodbye to the kids he had gotten to know was one of the hardest things he had ever done. The whole community came out for Skate Night to wish him well before he left.

He didn't miss the laughter of children long, however, as local Ys immediately recruited him prior to his finding his destiny with the Boys & Girls Club. The local Club had only been around for a few months and was serving only fifty kids in the little community center building in the park. A.Jaye knew there were many more kids in the neighborhood who needed a Club experience and asked to speak directly to the board of directors.

"I am used to working with a much bigger group of kids. I have some ideas to get more kids here, will you let me try?"

With their blessing, he went to every school in the surrounding area to meet with students and their parents to let them know how much fun they would have at the Club. The city park the Club was in had a reputation for rough activity, but he assured the parents that their kids would be safe, fed, and entertained. (After the Club increased membership and recognition, the park became a desirable place for families every day.)

That first summer, Club enrollment increased to 180 members, and the second summer to three hundred. A.Jaye said he prayed for sunny days so they could be outside. That was when the board of directors got serious about a capital campaign to raise funds for a building to meet the proven need. A.Jaye provided advice and support as the new Clubhouse was built over the next several years, dramatically increasing the number of kids they could serve and also providing spaces for more activities and enrichment opportunities.

At the height of all of this, the beloved leader suffered massive strokes. It was the Friday in June before the all-day summer programs at the Club were about to start. He later said he'd realized his body had been giving him signs, but like many young men who think they are invincible, he had ignored them. He said that after his mom died, he had quit taking good care of himself. He worked twelve-hour days, ate fast food, and went to bed with no time or interest in exercising.

A.Jaye was in the hospital for heart evaluation when he had two severe strokes. He couldn't walk. He couldn't talk. He even doubted his will to live until his daughter Rylea climbed up in his hospital bed to tell him she would always love him, no matter what condition he was in. That was when he decided to fight his way back.

Very unlike his pre-stroke self, A.Jaye became uncomfortable in crowds and hung onto his wife's shirt for security when they went out. He was embarrassed to talk in public and would point to items on the menu in restaurants for her to order for him.

With months of focus and practice, his physical therapists helped him learn to walk again. His speech pathologist helped him learn to speak clearly, advancing from simple-word flash cards to practicing giving speeches from behind a podium. His cardiologists taught him the importance of healthy eating and exercise. And fight back he did. A.Jaye became such a model patient that the American Heart Association shares a video with his story.

Get well cards from Club kids warmed his heart and added fuel to his fire to return.

Not until the next November, six months later, was A.Jaye able to come back to the Club. The kids were surprised and overjoyed to see him walking into the gym with the help of a cane and eighty pounds lighter. A large community gathering complete with NBA cheerleaders, balloons, and refreshments welcomed him back in style.

"Those kids, and our community, motivated me to fight my way back. I needed them more than they needed me," he told me years later.

A.Jaye celebrated his twenty-year anniversary as a professional staff member of the Boys & Girls Club in May of 2022. When you engage him in conversation now, there are no signs of those post-stroke insecurities or trouble speaking. In fact, he could talk to you all day about the long list of kids he has mentored over the years and has sometimes been a father figure to. He lights up as he tells you about the young lady who is completing her residency in medical school, the young man who owns a successful construction company in the northeast, or the group of little girls he helped with homework every day who will be seniors in high school next year.

SHARON GORDON LINTON

There simply is not enough time for A.Jaye to tell you all the stories of the thousands of kids he has helped, because the next group is running in the door!

When I reconnected with Sharon at Dunkin' Donuts three years after I had retired, it was as though no time had passed. Her "God is Big Enough" wristband reminded me how I had watched her act out her personal faith by nurturing the youngest Club members for many years.

"I am planting seeds every single day," she reminded me. "I like to work with the little ones to create the foundation for their growth at the Club. I become their anchor, and they know I care about them and will be watching out for them even as they get older. It's important to meet children where they are and help them pull themselves up. They can do anything. The sky is the limit when we show them good examples."

Sharon's "pull themselves up" expression is particularly fitting in that she has personally learned to adapt to being incapacitated on the left side of her body. When she was three months old, her mom accidently fell down a flight of stairs and dropped her. Her cracked skull resulted in her living with impacts of cerebral palsy for the rest of her life.

Sharon's disability has not prevented her from loving "her babies," however. "The Boys & Girls Club has my heart," she said. Sharon appreciates the organization's support and flexibility over her eighteen years as a beloved staff member. "They bought me a special chair," she said. "When I need to sit down, I sit down. If I need to take a few days off from time to time to build my strength, it's okay."

Sharon has a unique understanding of the challenges many kids come with to the Club, especially those in the foster care system. Sharon, her mom, and her two sisters fostered countless children when they lived in Yuma, Arizona. They lived in four houses next door to each other and worked together to provide opportunities and support for multiple children in the foster care system. She said at any given time, the four women cared for ten to twelve children.

When she moved to Oklahoma, Sharon became a foster parent again before adopting her sweet baby girl when she was two days old. She told me that her daughter's biological mother was addicted to drugs and alcohol, giving her baby a challenging start. As a teen, her daughter found a file with paperwork describing her biological mother's addictions and became very concerned about how that DNA history might impact her future. Sharon assured her that she could choose her own path, and at nineteen years old, she seems to be making positive choices as a very bright, creative, energetic young woman.

Sharon's eyes lit up when we talked about the Boys & Girls Club and I mentioned how Sergio had told me how much he enjoyed working with her as a junior staff member. She said Sergio's younger brother was her junior staff helper this past summer, and that it's been fun to see his younger siblings growing up in the Club as well.

In addition to providing a foundation for their time at the Club, Sharon's priority for the children in her group each year is for them to learn to read. She reminded me about the state law that decrees students cannot advance to fourth grade without passing third grade reading tests, and that mastering the basics of reading is so important to all their subsequent academic work. She lamented the trauma created when a child is held back, and the impact on self-esteem when students become taller than their classmates and continually feel the shame of not being able to read. She has always had phonics materials and a variety of books in the rooms where she worked, but she was especially happy when she got permission to move her classes into to the Club library.

Sharon and the first grade Club staff leader have started a Chef's Corner program, in which their kids get to prepare creative and healthy snacks on Fridays. Reading tasty recipes is one example of what BGCA would call "fun with a purpose." From my perspective, a recipe for a child's success starts with Sharon.

CHAPTER 9
Better than a Bon Jovi Concert

"There can be no keener revelation of a society's soul than the way in which it treats its children."

—Nelson Mandela

ADAN

Adan suddenly got very quiet. He tossed his head back on the tufted brocade fabric of the restaurant booth and sighed. "Life happens," he said. "Then I start remembering how these people affected me. It's great that we started talking about them, and it's so nice to know so many are still there. It's trippy in a sense that I can't explain, but it's a really nice feeling."

The senior in high school became nostalgic and joyful when we reconnected to talk about his earlier experiences at the Boys & Girls Club. Our lunchtime gathering ended with eighteen-year-old Adan insisting on buying his mom's and my lunch and planning to reunite soon with some of his favorite staff members and volunteers at the Club.

Adan was born in the US but had spent a good portion of his early years living with his grandparents in Peru. Compounding the fact that his grandparents spoke only Spanish, he had missed out on significant language development as an infant and toddler due to his enlarged tonsils and the related fluid in his ears that impaired his hearing. Once the health issues were surgically corrected, his mom said with a laugh, Adan never stopped talking!

With little command of the English language, his mom found work cleaning houses and office buildings in Oklahoma City and needed a place for her six-year-old son to be cared for after school and during school breaks. She enrolled him at the Boys & Girls Club and told me during our recent lunch together what a tremendous help that had been for her. She especially appreciated that the Club provided transportation from school so she didn't have to leave work in the middle of the day.

Even as a young child, Adan was unusually bright and enjoyed sharing stories about his love for the Boys & Girls Club. At only eight years old, he touted the benefits of the Club before a large gathering of Junior League ladies at a local country club, thanking them for their support. Dwarfed by the giant lectern, young Adan balanced on a chair to talk about the things he liked to do. He said he especially enjoyed hanging out in the computer lab and eating good snacks. The ladies laughed at his jokes and gave him a standing ovation, which prompted a deep bow on the outside and growing sense of accomplishment on the inside. When we talked years later, Adan told me how nervous he had been, but that he had enjoyed drawing the name of the winner of the League's raffle from a giant fishbowl of ticket stubs.

Soon after the event at the country club, the young ambassador again shared the spotlight at a media event and press conference announcing Dell Computer's technology grant. He talked about his love of computers and his earlier disappointment in the Club's antiquated, dysfunctional computer lab prior to its major transformation with Dell's financial support and army of volunteers. He convinced the audience that Dell's investment in state-of-the art technology for kids at the Club would open a world of opportunities and change lives. Since Adan plans to major in computer science in college and expressed high hopes of creating a better world through technology, I couldn't help but wonder how that expanded computer lab had equipped and motivated him.

At the recent lunch, Adan became the most animated when we talked about the staff and volunteers he had known and admired. While reminiscing about his experiences at the Club, he leaned back in the restaurant booth and started rapidly shooting out names of helpful adults he had gotten to know, asking first to hear how they were doing and, second, to know if they were still there.

- He remembered Linda making woven bracelets with him, then giving him the one she had made, and how that made him feel special.
- He said Wes, a volunteer, was his hero. Wes helped Adan feel calm after stressful days at school, and his kindness and generosity influenced who Adan is today.
- He mentioned Cedric, the bus driver who did not get irritated with Adan for calling him by the wrong name over and over for years. Adan said his twelve-year-old self apologized profusely once he realized his repeated error.
- He talked about what a great leader and mentor A.Jaye was, and how he helped resolve a couple of incidents that had affected Adan. One involved two boys taking Adan's cell phone out of a Club cubby while Adan was in karate. Video cameras mounted in all the rooms made it easy for staff to identify the culprits. Without raising his voice or threatening, A.Jaye counseled the two boys, successfully got Adan's cell phone returned, and created an important learning opportunity about honesty for all.
- He asked about Ms. Jackson and the Come Read with Me program he enjoyed through a partnership with the metropolitan library system.

When he and I met together at the Club a few days after our lunch, Adan seemed excited to have the opportunity to personally thank LaRissa for inviting him to be part of the Club choir, proudly telling her that because she recognized his musical talent, he now is a member of a competition choir at his high school. He enjoyed reminiscing about scouting with Sheila, who led the Club's Boy Scout troops on many camping adventures. She teased him about always wanting to have the same tent, and he teased her back about the multiple Boys & Girls Club staff shirts that she had decorated with fringe on the bottom.

AN EXCEPTIONAL MENTOR

But it was one chance meeting at the Club that particularly stands out and continues to enrich Adan's life in multiple ways. Cliff Hudson, the CEO of a national fast food restaurant chain, visited the Club one afternoon for a tour with one of his senior employees, Claudia San Pedro. His company was being honored for its support of the organization, and although he had been a Boys & Girls Club member as a child in Texas, he had never been to our local Club.

I had asked eight-year-old Adan to help lead the tour, after which he launched into a lively conversation in Spanish with Claudia about his experiences at home, school, and the Boys & Girls Club. Cliff and Claudia were impressed by Adan's precociousness, informative tour, and enthusiasm. That day was the beginning of a lifelong friendship.

Cliff and Claudia were concerned that Adan was not getting the best academic opportunities at the elementary school he attended. They asked to speak to his mom about transferring to a different school within the district, and Club staff assisted with the conversation that resulted in transferring Adan to another school. One advantage of this new school was that employees from the CEO's company routinely volunteered there. Cliff and his co-workers had consistent opportunities to check on Adan's progress while serving the student population in general. He quickly began to thrive.

Then came frightening news.

> "There were many important people there, but they treated me like I was the important one."

His mom had plans to move them to a suburban community with lower housing costs. He would be leaving the successful school experience and the repeated opportunities to see his beloved mentor. Cliff was so concerned about disrupting Adan's progress and their ability to stay connected that he located an affordable place nearby for them to live. Opportunities at the school and with his mentor remained intact. Cliff later coached Adan in choosing the best middle and high schools for his talents and interests, and has been involved recently with helping him explore college opportunities, resulting in his plans to start at the University of Science & Arts of Oklahoma in the fall.

One memorable experience Adan had with his mentor involved meeting former US president Bill Clinton at an event in Cliff's home. Adan told me that his mentor introduced him to others at the event as the "co-host," and that although there were many very important people there, they treated him like he was the important one. Few twelve-year-olds have the opportunity to have a face-to-face conversation with a US president. Adan told me the next week that it was even better than seeing Bon Jovi in concert!

Adan talked to me about being unaware of Cliff's importance in the community initially, but how he was drawn to him because he listened and cared. He said that Cliff, like staff and other volunteers at the Club, was good about letting him share his opinions and thoughts first before interjecting their own. He added that Cliff joining him for the Club's Thanksgiving dinners every year made those times extra special.

Cliff and Adan at a Club Thanksgiving dinner

Cliff and Adan at a college tour

Adan was able to publicly thank his mentor in a video shown at a community event.

"Ms. Jane asked me to lead a tour for some people," said Adan, "and I see this man standing there who was way taller than me. It was Mr. Cliff. I didn't know him. He was just a stranger to me, but then, we got to know each other and started playing pool and making lanyards. I thought in my brain, I was processing what a good person he was, how good Mr. Cliff was. Life was hard for me, honestly, and without him, I couldn't be where I am right now. He is a sincere blessing."

CHAPTER 10
The Family Business

"I have a dream too. But it's about singing and dancing and making people happy. That's the kind of dream that gets better the more people you share it with. And I found a whole bunch of people who share the same dream, and that kind of makes us a family."

—Kermit the Frog, *Before You Leap*

When I visited with former Club member AnaMarie as an adult, they explained their interest in helping me with this book by reminding me that "even after you've graduated and moved on, people at the Boys & Girls Club are still family." Indeed, if you spend enough time at any Boys & Girls Club, you will hear someone refer to the people there as a family. Club kids, staff, and volunteers support one another in unique and meaningful ways. They share the dream of better futures for themselves, each other, and the community.

With a sense of belonging and gratitude, it is not unusual for Boys & Girls Clubs' alums to become staff members, volunteers, donors, and leaders of their local organizations. They continue to find ways to invest in the "family business." They know from personal experience the struggles that young people face and the difference that acceptance, encouragement, opportunities, and positive mentors and role models can make. More than half of them say that being part of the Boys & Girls Club family saved their lives. I was honored to get to know both kids and adults whose stories made that statistic real, and I wanted to know more about their circumstances as children and how they continue to pass on the Boys & Girls Club family values.

Hope for America's Youth

RICK NAGEL

"No matter what happens in my life, it will never be as bad as when I was a kid. I have drawn strength from that perspective," Rick told me as he grabbed a quick bite of pizza during a few spare minutes between his daughter's soccer matches.

Living in Nebraska, Rick was only nine years old when his thirty-five-year-old father died suddenly from a heart attack. To make matters even more tragic, soon after, his mom was diagnosed with Guillain-Barre syndrome and hospitalized for nearly a year. After his mom became ill, the first stop for Rick and his younger brother was a temporary foster home, followed by an expected "permanent" home—in which the boys were severely physically abused. They then were jostled among eight foster families in one short year.

A rare bright spot while living with one of the foster families came when Rick walked into the local Boys & Girls Club. He had no idea how entering those blue doors would begin to foreshadow his lifelong dedication to the Boys & Girls Club family business.

The boys' mom's release from the hospital provided no fairy-tale ending. Never fully recovered from her disease, her disabilities made it impossible to find satisfactory work to provide for her family. They lived on government subsidies and moved every few months, often at the whim of various men his mom brought home. At only ten years old, Rick started mowing lawns and doing other odd jobs just to help provide for their basic needs.

When he was thirteen, Rick deeply gashed his hand while carving a pumpkin for Halloween. He could tell he was badly hurt and begged his mom to take him to a doctor, but instead, she and her then boyfriend yelled at him about not being able to afford it. That became a defining moment. Rick said he made up his mind right then that when he grew up, he would make enough money to take care of himself and those he loved.

Fortuitously, the family ended up in Ft. Smith, Arkansas, when Rick started high school. It was the Boys & Girls Club there that changed the trajectory of his life. "I moved out of the house at the start of my senior year. I was a poor kid with no sense of home. I didn't trust anybody. I was ashamed about everything in my past and what I was dealing with," Rick said. "The Boys & Girls Club helped me face it all and turn it into good. My circumstances didn't define me. I could create a better life, and they were there to help me."

The Club Unit Director Alvin Matlock and Club Executive Director Jerry Glidewell saw promise in seventeen-year-old Rick, and encouraged him to do two things that cleared pathways toward that better life: (1) compete to become the Club's Youth of the Year, and (2) apply for a Phillips 66 engineering college scholarship.

Motivated, Rick told his compelling story and became that Club's and, within a few months, the State of Arkansas's Youth of the Year, later advancing to the Southwest Region Youth of the Year, and ultimately, first runner-up for the national honor. Being runner-up for BGCA's national Youth of the Year rewarded Rick beautifully, as the winner played basketball for his university and was unable to make several of the scheduled speaking engagements. His unavailability created the path for Rick's front-and-center involvement. Rick jumped at the chance to sharpen his presentation skills and build lasting relationships. At eighteen years old, he met President George Bush and Vice President Dan Quail in the Oval Office. Now, as an adult with an office in Washington, DC, he told me he thinks about that experience every time he walks by the hotel where he stayed as a teen representing BGCA.

Receiving the Phillips 66 scholarship through the Club also allowed him to dream of a college education that would otherwise have been impossible with no family support. When he went to Bartlesville, Oklahoma, to receive the scholarship, Pete Silas, CEO of Phillips Petroleum, asked Rick if he had considered attending the University of Oklahoma (OU). Rick said that he had looked only as far as colleges in Arkansas, thinking he needed to stay close to watch over his disabled mom and younger brother. But by the time he got home from that trip, there was a message on his apartment phone from the dean of Engineering at OU, encouraging him to study there. Rick was shocked that the CEO of a major international company had taken the time to call the dean, resulting in his recruitment call with additional financial support. OU won his heart.

As an excited recent high school graduate on his way to a major university in another state, he loaded up his beat-up old car with extra oil and tools and headed to Norman. He told me that he had serious doubts that he would even make it to campus. He definitely never imagined that thirty years later, the governor of the state would name him to serve on OU's Board of Regents!

Rick graduated from OU in December 1994, and three months later, he got a call from a group of people starting a new Boys & Girls Club organization in Oklahoma City. They asked him to serve as a member of their founding board of directors.

"I was really taken aback by that invitation," he said. "I had just graduated from college, had a new job and no money, but I felt obligated to give back to the organization that had done so much for me. I have always had a deep sense of loyalty to the people who helped me along the way."

Rick became the youngest board member of the newly formed Boys & Girls Club organization that, twenty-nine years later, serves over sixteen thousand youth. He is the one exception to term limits on the local board of directors, but his time, energy, and commitments do not stop there. He founded and continues to head the state alliance for the over twenty-five Club organizations and ninety Club sites across the state, and he also has the distinguished honor to serve as a National Trustee for Boys & Girls Clubs of America.

Economic disparities in the US are an issue close to Rick's heart, and he believes the ZIP code someone is born in should not determine their access to basic supports. He is convinced that strengthening Boys & Girls Clubs is a meaningful way to level the playing field. Among the many things he has done for the local Club is establishing a scholarship fund through a local community foundation. Preference is shown for scholarships to Club members who plan to study science, technology, engineering, or math, just like the one he received as a Club kid.

He supports the local Club's fundraising events, especially Flight for Futures, which takes place in an airplane hangar. With his personal jet parked in the corner, Club members have an opportunity to explore the interior and get a glimpse of the great futures they can have if they make good choices. I invited current Club kids to tour his jet at a recent event and marveled at their oohs and aahs and excitement over the realization that someone "like them" was able to have this kind of success.

"When you aren't sure where you are going to sleep tomorrow night, or if you'll eat dinner later, you aren't thinking about your future as a grown-up. I want to give kids a reason and opportunity to dream bigger than they normally would and make sure they've got the resources to be successful and self-sustaining adults," Rick said. "We help along their journey through youth so that they're making healthy choices, that they have support to achieve academic excellence, and that they're going to be good citizens. We want them to graduate with opportunities for the future, whatever that might be, including going to college, technical school, or right into the workforce or the military."

Oklahoma County Youth of the Year Anthony with Rick Nagel

"The complex web of issues we face from generational poverty are not going to solve themselves," Rick added. "There is no other organization with the scale, talent, level of programming, and track record to address the challenges our country faces than the Boys & Girls Clubs. I sincerely hope everyone who reads this will become inspired to volunteer and support his great cause."

The proud Boys & Girls Club alum is CEO and managing partner of Acorn Growth Companies, a private equity firm focused on aerospace, defense, intelligence, and space investments with offices in Oklahoma City, Washington, DC, and London. His work requires weekly travel across the globe, yet for him, leaving a legacy through Boys & Girls Club kids remains top of mind.

JENNIFER FOGG LICKTEIG

Jenn had been with the wrong girls at the wrong time and faced consequences for her actions. As a teen in California, she and her friends were trespassing through houses under construction. One of the girls left the faucet running in an upstairs bathroom, causing the duplex to flood and hundreds of thousands of dollars in damages. The judge in Jenn's court case sentenced her to two thousand hours of community service. Jenn had a bad attitude in general, and only after every other service organization declined to accept her did she find the Boys & Girls Club.

"I hated those early days. I really thought the kids that went to that Club were beneath me," she told me recently. Knowing her now as a remarkably inclusive and compassionate adult, it's hard to imagine Jenn as such an arrogant teen.

While doing her community service in California, Club staff gave her dirty assignments like taking trash to the dumpster and keeping the parking lot swept clean. She did not see herself having anything in common with the kids and teens who went to the Club. One extremely cold and rainy day, young Jenn was particularly angry as she picked up trash in the parking lot. Hearing her mutter profanities, the maintenance worker at the Club approached her with a suggestion. "You know," he said. "If you would put a smile on your face and display a better attitude, we might be able to find community service work for you to do inside the building, where it is warm and dry."

Jenn took that recommendation to heart, and it changed her life.

Inside the Club, she not only found people who cared, but she developed a passion and purpose for serving others. She continued as a Club member after her community service hours were complete, building friendships and goals for a more fulfilling, crime-free life. She also discovered she was actually just like the other kids at the Club. "The realization that I made bad choices because of issues I was facing at home put things into perspective when I started seeing the kids there as just like me," she said.

Twenty years later, after she had become the CEO of three companies in California and Oklahoma, and had led teams of over ten-thousand employees, a young girl's speech at a Boys & Girls Club gala event brought a tidal wave of memories and emotions to the surface. When Addie, the local Youth of the Year, spoke of how the Club had impacted her life, Jenn started remembering how she had turned her life around as a teenager in that distant Club.

She contacted me and offered to provide scholarship money for our Youths of the Year each year. She didn't just write a check, however: she met with each winner over a nice lunch and shared her own story of inspiration and gratitude. Her support for the organization evolved over the years and included becoming a volunteer member of the board of directors, making a significant challenge match at a later fundraising event, and giving valued advice to Club leadership.

Jenn talks about the realization that everyone has problems, many bigger than your own. She said her time at the Club set a foundation for how to treat others with empathy, compassion, and grace. "Being part of the Boys & Girls Club family business not only makes us better leaders, but better human beings," she said.

CARL ANDERSON

When we met at a local diner recently, twenty-two-year-old Carl agreed with my memory that when he was a young boy at the Memorial Park Club, he often got in trouble for sneaking away from his group to shoot hoops in the gym. He also admitted that learning to control his anger was an important lesson.

"I started going to the Club when I was six years old and have been there every day since," he said with a smile. "During the summers as a kid, I was there from 7:00 a.m. until 7:00 p.m. There were lots of fun things to do, and the staff members made it like home."

When he became a teen, Carl worked with a couple of amazing staff and volunteers in a program called Parks in Focus. The Parks in Focus program was started by the Udall Foundation and was designed to encourage young people to become engaged in nature through the art of photography. The program provided participants with their own inexpensive point-and-shoot cameras and took them on field trips to parks around the state where they found a variety of settings for taking pictures of nature. Carl had a superb eye and shot some beautiful photographs. Our administrative staff even turned one of his photos into a stunning notecard we used to thank donors.

Once Carl found his connection, he became an outstanding Club member, followed by becoming a junior staff member in his teens and an exemplary staff person after graduating from high school. He told me during our recent visit that he plans to start college next semester and major in child psychology, because while working at the Club, he has become even more aware of the many problems kids face. He thinks parental neglect is the biggest problem, and that all too often he hears kids talk about not feeling loved.

Carl works daily with a fellow staff member to serve fifty-one third grade Club members and especially loves being with them when they experience a new activity or see something for the first time. During the school year, they have Power Hour homework help every day, and he gives members writing prompts to help them learn to express themselves. He told me about summer field trips that included River Sport, White Water Bay, Science Museum of Oklahoma, Oklahoma City Zoo, Blue Zoo Aquarium, and others, and mentioned that most Club kids wouldn't otherwise have those types of experiences.

Carl's staff mentor LaRissa told me a story about a child getting hurt in the park behind the Club while playing football with his group.

He accidentally ran into a metal pole and cut his head, resulting in an immediate call to 9-1-1. After calling for an ambulance, LaRissa made the call to the boy's mom, fearful about how she would take the news. LaRissa heard the injured child's mom's audible sigh of relief once she reassured her that Carl had been with her son the whole time.

"Well, if Mr. Carl is with him, I know he is okay," the mom replied. When I asked Carl about that experience, he smiled broadly and said he remembers it like it was yesterday.

Powerful, transformational legacies like those that Rick, Jenn, and Carl are creating through the family business show how good investments multiply, serving first one generation and then another and another.

CHAPTER 11
When All Else Fails, Love Remains

> *"Some of the most told stories are the ones that don't end well, the ones that are beautiful because someone laid it all on the line, was brave and vulnerable and submitted to the human condition. If that's your story, it's time to stop running from it and start taking pride in the fact that you were strong enough to let love through."*
>
> —Brianna Wiest

MARY KATE

I had retired a few months earlier and was sitting at home reading the newspaper early one cold November morning when the call from an unrecognized number appeared on my phone. The woman on the other end shared the shocking news: "A young lady was abandoned at the front door of the Boys & Girls Club in the bitter cold at 4:30 this morning. When the sun came up, she dragged her four heavy bags of belongings across the park to our office building, so we let her in. She remembered your number and thought you might help."

I knew immediately that it must be Mary Kate. She had a long history of abandonment. After horrific sexual, physical, and mental abuse, this sweet nineteen-year-old had been a ward of the state since she was five years old. As she neared her eighteenth birthday, the notorious age of being cast out of the state foster care system, she had moved to Texas to live with a great-aunt. The previously estranged relative continually put her down and consistently told her that no one wanted her. She called Mary Kate shameful names and hit her. That relationship exacerbated the lifelong challenges for a child who only wanted to be loved.

Mary Kate later told me that the night before the early-morning phone call, she and her great-aunt had gotten into a fist fight, and her great-aunt kicked her out of the house. They loaded Mary Kate's few belongings—some clothes, stuffed animals, CD player, and miscellaneous memorabilia—into a beat-up station wagon and drove several hours across the Texas-Oklahoma state line toward Oklahoma City. The great-aunt threated to drop her on the side of the highway at the state line, but Mary Kate begged her to at least take her to the front porch of the Boys & Girls Club she had attended as a child.

She had no phone and was desperate. She waited on the Club's front porch until daybreak, and then walked a city block over to the office building where our administrative offices had been, hoping to find someone to help. She didn't know that I had retired or that the Club's offices had moved to a different building. When she didn't find a familiar office or face, she asked for help in the attorney's office. She remembered my cell number as a lifeline, so the office receptionist called and asked permission to hand her the phone. Mary Kate started crying as soon as she heard my voice. "Can you please come get me?" she pleaded.

I quickly dressed and started the twenty-minute drive to pick her up. My mind was racing in search for potential options and people in my network who might be able to help her find semi-permanent housing. Leaders of other United Way partner agencies came to mind. On the drive, I called Jennifer Goodrich, the director of Pivot, a local shelter for homeless teens and young adults. It was before business hours, so I left a voice message with my own plea for assistance. I pulled up to the office building to greet Mary Kate with a long and tearful hug.

"The Boys & Girls Club has always been my home," she told me through her tears. "It was the only place I knew to go."

> "The Boys & Girls Club has always been my home. It was the only place I knew to go."

She was scared. She was cold. She felt unloved.

Thankfully, Jennifer returned my call quickly. She invited me to bring Mary

Kate to the Pivot shelter at 4:00 p.m. I was so relieved by her gracious and immediate support. It seemed to solve a huge logistical issue, if not the deeper emotional issues that I knew Mary Kate was facing after being abandoned by her family yet again. With housing likely secured, I decided to try to give Mary Kate a day filled with love. I wanted to at least attempt to counteract the traumatic rejection she had experienced. We started with a warm and hearty breakfast downtown. Then we spent the rest of the day connecting with people who had given her light, hope, and love earlier in her life. Once the Boys & Girls Club doors opened, I took her to reconnect with familiar staff members, all of whom welcomed her with open arms. One of her foster moms, a woman who had been good to her and whom she remembered fondly, invited us to come by for a visit.

That afternoon, Pivot provided a bed and promised to connect Mary Kate with a case manager who would help her find work and/or educational opportunities and eventually a more permanent place to live. I was relieved she would have a safe place to sleep and be given breakfasts and dinners daily. I hoped that she would make new friends, knowing that some of the young people at the shelter might relate to the trauma she had experienced.

A couple of weeks later, our family invited Mary Kate to spend Thanksgiving Day with us. She enjoyed the day away from the shelter, but at the end of the day, she made a surprising request: She asked me to take her to the apartment where her mom and stepdad were living before she returned to Pivot. I was shocked because I had been under the impression that Mary Kate had had little if any contact with her mom after she was taken from her home as a little girl. It turned out that her mom had seen the great-aunt's Facebook post about throwing Mary Kate out of her house and "dumping" her at the Boys & Girls Club in Oklahoma City. After seeing that post, her mom reconnected with her long-estranged daughter via Facebook messenger. When we got to their apartment, her mom profusely thanked me for rescuing her on that frigid morning she was left at the Club. Mary Kate's desire to reconnect with her mom, even after the countless injustices she had endured, demonstrated her desperate need to be part of a family at whatever cost.

Mary Kate was only five years old when she was first taken into state custody after being sexually assaulted by her father. She started attending the Boys & Girls Club around that time, and she usually was able to participate in Club activities even as she was moved from one foster home to the next, giving her a thread of stability as she started her life over again and again. By the time she graduated from high school, she had lived in seven foster homes and four group homes, never finding a forever home. She was a teenager when I first got to know her, and it was obvious from her roller-coaster moods that the trauma she had experienced at a young age had continued to wreak havoc on her mental health.

One afternoon, I saw Mary Kate's case worker leaving the Club in a panic. Mary Kate had been kicked out of her foster home, and the state agency didn't have any place for her to go. My heart ached as I watched Mary Kate walk around and around in circles in our spacious Clubhouse lobby as other Club members came and went. She was visibly distraught, wringing her hands and sighing under her breath as she paced the floor. I asked the case worker how I could help, and she implored me to consider letting Mary Kate stay in my home for a few nights while the state found a more permanent foster care solution. I wanted to help calm her down and naively thought that since I was the leader of a Boys & Girls Club and had passed multiple background checks at the state and federal level, that I would be permitted to take her home with me at the end of my work day. That was not the case. The case worker insisted that she must go through a multi-step process of getting my family approved for temporary foster care, even for a brief stay. They ran new background checks on my husband and me, called references, conducted an in-person home visit, and completed mountains of paperwork before finally bringing the exhausted and frightened fifteen-year-old to our house just after midnight.

It's quite complicated to try to care for a child with a history of so much trauma. Mary Kate often had emotional outbursts that put foster families on guard. During her stay at my house, I found her rummaging through drawers in common areas and bedrooms, apparently looking for items she might want. Sometimes she would ask if she could keep "treasures" she found; other times, she just took them. Her other foster parents observed similar patterns. The consensus seemed to be that she was reacting to the scarcity in her own life by stealing from homes where there seemed to be such great abundance. It was frustrating, of course, but a pattern that was understandable given the unthinkably difficult life she'd lived to date.

In other ways, however, Mary Kate was a courteous and conscientious guest. She adored our dog and cat and offered to help prepare meals. She frequently greeted me, my family, and others with a big smile, shiny blue eyes, and warm embrace. She was quick to say "I love you." While at the Boys & Girls Club, she eagerly connected with staff and tried to develop friendships with her peers. She desperately wanted to give and receive love wherever she went. State-sponsored adoption events, year after year, only fueled her ever-present feelings of rejection. She left each event without a "forever" home. Despite these crushing disappointments, she remained hopeful that she might find a match with that illusive family. When none appeared, you could see heartbreak in her tears.

After the two-week stay at my house, I helped the state place her with a compassionate family I'd known, where she lived happily for a time. After several months, however, a couple of unfortunate things happened. First, Mary Kate used one of the foster parent's credit cards without permission to order $2,000 worth of video games online. Second, her foster mom told me that even more problematic and frightening for them was discovering the impact on her elderly mom who lived with them. She said her mother, who was physically immobile, had been waking up to discover Mary Kate sneaking in her room in the middle of the night looking for jewelry, phones, or anything she might want.

Feeling that it was no longer acceptable for Mary Kate to live with them, the foster mom said they followed the protocol established by the state agency to move her out. When Mary Kate got off the bus from school the next day, she was shocked to see that her foster family had stacked all of her belongings in the hall by the front door. It was an abrupt and excruciatingly painful end to the best opportunity she had had to connect with a long-term and loving family. As pre-arranged, her case worker brought her to my house to spend the night, and all I could do was hold her in my arms as she sobbed uncontrollably. The next day, she moved to a group home in a town two hours away.

These and other memories of Mary Kate flooded back to me as I started writing this book. Most of the young people I wanted to feature in these pages could easily be described as "success stories." They had been our Club's Youths of the Year and/or had managed to make strides academically and socially that many people thought unimaginable. Because I was CEO and primarily focused on administrative duties rather than supervising Club members, those kids were the ones I had the most opportunity to get to know. I listened to them practice their speeches, celebrated them at banquets, and cheered them on as they attended and won competitions. But their stories are only part of the overall picture. I couldn't write about "my" kids at the Club without including the story of Mary Kate, whose traumatic life haunts me to this day. Mentorship can make such a difference for so many kids, but a compassionate mentor simply is not always enough.

As I sat down to write, I thought about the last time I had heard from Mary Kate. It had been three years since she had been abandoned on the front porch of the Boys & Girls Club and moved into Pivot's youth shelter. I knew that she had gotten into a fist fight with another resident, and that she was told to leave a few weeks after I had seen her at Thanksgiving. We had fallen in and out of touch after that, but she would sometimes call me when she got a different cell phone number (which happened frequently). She reached out in the fall of 2023 to tell me she was living in Norman, a college town south of Oklahoma City, and agreed to meet me at Norman's public library.

On the forty-five-minute drive to the library, my mind raced with questions. Where was Mary Kate living? Had she reconnected with family? And, related to research for this book, had her experiences at the Boys & Girls Club helped her, or was she so haunted by demons of the past and layers of rejection that she'd completely buried her creative spirit and hidden her bright blue eyes from the world?

When I got to the library, I was pleasantly surprised to see how good she looked. Her shiny black hair had been given a fresh and sassy haircut, and her eyes still sparkled. She and her boyfriend had been spending nights in a shelter called A Friend's House and most of their daytime hours at the library. They passed the days by listening to audio books from the Overlanders series or hanging out by the 3D printers or the library's guinea pigs. She gave me a tight and lengthy hug before we sat down on the cushy purple chairs across from the floor-to-ceiling glass walls overlooking the multi-story floating-paper sculpture in front of the building. She was excited to hear about my book project, and she told me she wanted her story to be part of it. I questioned whether to include her story in this book because of its sensitive nature, but in the end, I felt like the respectful thing to do was honor Mary Kate's wish to be seen and heard.

I was thrilled to get some joyous news from her. Mary Kate and her boyfriend had met at Pivot three years earlier, and she said they planned to get married the following week. She invited my family to the wedding, which would take place at the shelter. I showed up on the expected wedding day with my husband, son, and one of Mary Kate's former foster moms. I was so happy for Mary Kate—that she'd met someone to love who loved her back, and that they wanted to share that commitment with all of us. But when we arrived at the shelter, there was no sign of them. We spent some time looking around and talking to staff, but eventually realized there would not be a wedding that day. We left, and I called Mary Kate on the way out of town. She answered, to my surprise, and begged us to stop by the library to see her fiancé and her.

When we got to the library, she told us she had run out of money and that the priest wasn't available that day. While they seemed committed to one another, they didn't have the resources or capacity to go through the steps of procuring a marriage license or arranging for an appropriate official to conduct the ceremony. I'd brought a gift for her and a childhood photo album that she'd left behind with the foster parent I knew. We looked through the images of her past together. There were pictures of her when she was very young with her older sister and younger brother, and a few in later years at state agency events for kids in foster care. It crushed me to see these glimpses of a sweet, beautiful, and innocent little girl with her whole life ahead of her. I left with a sense of despair and foreboding.

Three months later, I got yet another desperate call for help. Mary Kate said she and her fiancé had been living outdoors in a field in Norman for the past couple of months, and she was at the end of her rope. Would I please put them up in a hotel for one week until her next Social Security check arrived? After arranging for a one-week stay, I began feverously looking for a better long-term option for my young friend.

Again, friendships made with other United Way Agency organization directors provided awareness of possible resources. Neighborhood Services Organization (NSO) provides rental assistance and housing, and Director Stacey Ninness and her team were quick to respond. They scheduled an interview for Mary Kate to be considered for a special apartment building for single women who had mental illness diagnoses and had been homeless. It seemed like the perfect long-term solution for Mary Kate, and I was ecstatic at the thought of her being in this safe and warm facility with consistent support. After the affirming interview with NSO, she said, "I love you," as she got out of my car to stay with her stepfather a few nights while her application could be approved and her apartment made ready.

> "You can give them resources, wisdom, and love, but ultimately their success is up to them. I had to learn to give up control. I had to be confident that I did my part and I did it well, but I couldn't give up on others just because things didn't always go as I had wished for some."
> —Wes Haddox

Then she disappeared. She didn't answer my persistent phone calls or texts. During the interview, she had disclosed to the intake worker that her boyfriend had been abusive and was angry that she was considering living in a shelter that would take only single women, not men or romantic couples. Mary Kate had told me earlier that her boyfriend had blocked my phone number from her phone so that we couldn't be in contact, so I tried calling from other numbers. It was no use. I feared for her safety, so I filed a missing-person report. Several days later, police confirmed that she had been seen with a young man at a pawn shop in Norman. They closed the case.

As I write in early 2024, temperatures in Oklahoma have dropped to one-degree Fahrenheit. I don't know where Mary Kate is, and I still worry about her. I regret giving her back her childhood photo album, knowing that those beloved images of her past likely have been lost in the shuffle of shelters and degrees of homelessness. It is heartbreaking and perplexing to mentor and love another person, only to witness firsthand their inability to choose a life that might offer a chance at security, safety, and love. Research indicates that repeated trauma, particularly at a young age, can rewire a person's brain, actually causing them to seek chaos rather than calm. Chaos is what they know.

Mary Kate's life is her own, and I must accept the decisions that she makes for herself. Still, I can't help but mourn what could have been—what could have been if Mary Kate had not been so horribly abused as an infant; what could have been if she had not been passed from foster home to foster home; what could have been if she'd had the chance to learn what a wonderful young woman she is and can be; and, finally, what could have been if she'd learned to love herself. There is still time for her to come to that realization, of course, but I regret that any child's path should be this difficult to travel.

Being a mentor can be (and usually is) life-affirming, energizing, and joyful. A mentor can be the spark that helps another person realize their potential. Those situations are inspiring to watch, and to write about. But it's also true that sometimes it is just not enough to overcome the cruelness and inequities that exist in our world. The trick for mentors is to not give up—to believe that change is possible and to continue to believe in the power of genuine connections.

While Mary Kate's present and future are uncertain and rife with horrendous challenges, I take comfort in knowing for certain that the Boys & Girls Club provided a safe and loving environment for her to spend her out-of-school time as a child and teen, and that her life was enriched by many multi-year, positive, life-affirming relationships that she wouldn't otherwise have had, including mine. Her Boys & Girls Club family does love her and has shown her that she is worthy of love. I pray someday she will believe it.

CHAPTER 12
Volunteer Keys

"There is always light. If only we're brave enough to see it. If only we're brave enough to be it."

—Amanda Gorman, US National Youth Poet Laureate

"Volunteers don't get paid, not because they're worthless, but because they're priceless."

—Sherry Anderson

While I felt like it was important to share, the relationship I have with Mary Kate clearly goes beyond a typical mentor-mentee relationship, and I would not want readers to think that level of commitment is expected. Thankfully, being a successful mentor is nearly always much less time-consuming and intense and can offer significant rewards for both the mentee and mentor. My experiences volunteering in Oklahoma City public schools while at ACOG were more light-hearted, yet lit my passion for working with youth and led me to my interest in becoming part of the Boys & Girls Clubs' extended family. Thinking about that continuum of involvement, I wondered what lessons about mentorship could be learned from a few of the volunteers who gave of themselves to kids at our Club. As part of my quest for answers, I asked them why they had chosen to donate their precious time and what insights they had to share.

DONNA LEFTWICH

Donna lost her sense of self and purpose when she was diagnosed with multiple sclerosis (MS). The disease hit her painfully and abruptly hard at the beginning, forcing her unexpectedly to abandon a longtime career in merchandizing.

"I thought I would never retire," Donna told me. She had loved her work and believed she had many good years ahead of her; she was devastated by the diagnosis and the lack of direction. She later became convinced that God had sent her to LaRissa, who was the Boys & Girls Clubs' volunteer coordinator at the time.

Donna said that raising her daughter had made her aware of challenges that all parents have, regardless of socioeconomic status. There always is concern about what to do with children after school. She knew, however, that those challenges were even more difficult for families who struggled financially to provide even the basics for their kids. Donna loves children and felt led to make a difference during that after-school time of the day.

"I had grown up in a privileged family with a mother and snacks waiting at home for me every day after school. I had a built-in adult who cared about my education and my future, and I had taken that for granted. I had no idea what to expect as a volunteer when I started going to the Boys & Girls Club, having had no direct experience like this before. I felt completely unqualified but learned that all you needed was to be present... with love," she said.

"I only want to talk about the gifts received, not given," Donna told me when I called to talk about her time as a volunteer. "Life always has blessings you never expected, and that's what I feel about the Boys & Girls Club. It's such a rich place."

"Just watching them run in off their buses after school was so great. Boys & Girls Club was their place, and it became my place with them," Donna said. She explained that they knew this was where they could get positive attention from a caring adult, a healthy snack, and a variety of fun activities. Many of them lived in situations where the adults were struggling to survive and didn't have the time to give them the one-on-one attention they craved.

Homework time at the Club is called Power Hour, and Donna quickly became known as "Ms. Donna, the Power Hour Girl." She said she was exposed to "such angels," both staff and children. She started with the "littles," as she called the kindergartners, and advanced with that same group as they got older, year after year.

Volunteer Keys

She told me about one boy whose father picked him up every day and how she was inspired by how intentional the father was about making sure that his son was taking advantage of all that the Club offered.

Then there was six-year-old Noah, who really struggled with his behavior. One day, as Donna arrived, Noah was in time-out for misbehaving, so she took the opportunity to connect with him in a special way. She asked him if he knew that NBA star Russell Westbrook, who was with the OKC Thunder at the time, had just had a baby and what the baby's name was. He was so excited when he learned Russell had named his baby Noah and said, "I wish Russell was my dad." Donna talked about the positive influence many of the Thunder players provided, especially since some of them had been "Club kids" themselves in their youth. Westbrook's Why Not Foundation provided a good example of how to give back with support of Thanksgiving celebrations, scholarships, and other activities at the Club.

Donna recalled the attorney who volunteered doing science projects with the kids, the little ballerinas dancing with instructors from the local ballet company, and all the other high-quality programming available for kids at the Club.

"There are so many blessings in that place. The kids knew they could go there and find answers to their questions and needs. Knowing where to go was half the battle." She observed the older Club members learning how to be involved in the broader community and how the teens who identified as LGBTQ+ found their comfort and confidence among accepting and encouraging staff, volunteers, and peers.

Her generous heart created opportunities for staff as well, evidenced clearly when she donated her own car to a beloved staff person who rode his bicycle to get to work every day, rain or shine, frigid or steaming.

The faithful volunteer showed up every week and enjoyed watching the kids grow through the various seasons at the Club. When asked why other people should get involved, Donna said simply, "Because the kids need them!"

WES HADDOX

"I think people think of the Boys & Girls Club as just a place where underserved kids go, but to an extent, as a longtime volunteer, I am a product of the Boys & Girls Club as well. I wear that as a badge of honor," said Wes, a wise young man with a huge heart.

What started out as a three-day directive from his former boss turned into a lifetime commitment for Wes. He had been working as an intern at the statewide Center of Nonprofits, when his mentor there suggested he volunteer at one of the local nonprofits for a few days while she was out of town. Although he didn't really think he liked children, he chose the Boys & Girls Club because it was one of her favorites.

"Before those three days, I thought kids were messy, self-centered, and whiny, but that place is magical," he said. "Important things happened in that bright Clubhouse, and I knew I wanted to go back. I had recently moved to town, and to be honest, I was lonely. In a selfish way, being at the Club filled me up when I saw I could help someone else. Those three days changed everything," he said.

> "I think people think of the Boys & Girls Club as just a place where underserved kids go, but to an extent, as a longtime volunteer, I am a product of the Boys & Girls Club as well. I wear that as a badge of honor."

"I immediately saw the need, but at first, I questioned who I was to think I could help. I had come from what I considered to be a more stable background, but quickly learned that didn't matter. The kids just craved someone being present, to listen to them."

Wes began to realize that he had been discounting or ignoring his own struggles growing up. Many of the teens at the Boys & Girls Club grew up without a father figure, and Wes had been estranged from his biological father. His stepfather was a big part of his life but worked long hours as the CEO of a large company. Wes said he had experienced something called shadow syndrome, which he defined as a child thinking he or she can't live up to the accomplishments or image of one of their parents.

"When I was in high school, I was in the car with my stepdad, talking about my failing grades in math, and I made the comment 'I will never be good enough to be a CEO like you.' My stepdad slammed on the breaks and exclaimed emphatically: 'Don't you ever compare yourself to me or anyone else! You are free to find your own path and purpose.'"

That experience and message had a real impact on Wes, and it serves as one of the principal tenants of conversations and relationships with his mentees at the Boys & Girls Club.

Wes believes that most kids grow up with some role or image attached to them based on the adults in their lives. For Club kids, those roles can relate to unattainable or sometimes unhealthy expectations such as becoming an NBA star, having millions of social media followers, or joining a gang like their parents or extended family.

"They often see post-high-school options to be college or nothing. There are lots of other perfectly good options like technology centers. I encourage them to reach for their dreams and try to metaphorically slam the breaks of self-doubt for these kids so they can find their own paths."

Wes has occasionally struggled with depression and shares his experiences to help his mentees talk about mental health and the value of expressing themselves. By opening up about his challenges, he helps them put a name to some of their own feelings and better work through them. It helps to have someone listen. One of his mentees experienced significant panic attacks but didn't know what they were. Giving them a label and talking through possible remedies was invaluable for overcoming them.

"Mental health challenges can make people feel all alone. They can put their head in the sand, but someone normalizing and validating their feelings can help them get to a healthier place," said Wes.

Wes has demonstrated the value of long-term commitment to multiple teens but admits that the results aren't always what are hoped for. "You can give them resources, wisdom, and love, but ultimately their success is up to them. I had to learn to give up control. I had to be confident that I did my part and I did it well, but I couldn't give up on others just because things didn't always go as I had wished for some."

The extraordinary young man continues to volunteer at the Club weekly and has also joined the organization's board of directors.

SUZANNE BREEDLOVE

Suzanne shared with me her concerns about the racial divisions in our country and how volunteers of various ethnicities are especially important to create positive relationships that bridge those cultural divides. "There are good people of every color in our world, and we are all put on Earth to help each other," she said.

She was drawn to volunteer at the Boys & Girls Clubs because she loves kids and was missing the opportunity to be around her stepchildren after her husband passed away. "I had seven stepchildren and thirty-one grandchildren, but lost regular contact with them after he was gone," she said.

"At first, the kids at the Boys & Girls Club didn't trust me. They were cautious and reserved. Each week when I came back, they warmed up more and more, until finally they greeted me in swarms, begging, 'Read to me! Read to me!'"

She emphasized the importance of commitment and consistency on the part of volunteers. "If you say you're going to be there, you better be there. These kids were hanging on my every word. They haven't always been told the truth, and it is important to not let them down."

Just giving them attention made such a difference by letting them know how important they were. She could see it when their faces lit up, and how wonderful it was to see the spark in their eyes when they were learning something new.

Suzanne said she could tell that while many Club members came from loving, supportive families, some of them were not getting their needs met at home. She recognized those living in troubling situations. They didn't want to leave at the end of the day, and they were quiet and withdrawn. And, occasionally, children disclosed that they were being abused at home, creating a need for Club staff to notify authorities.

Even with that short amount of time with the kids each week, she could see them come out of their shells, which she viewed as such a blessing. Suzanne said it took some of the kids a while to understand the rules at the Club, in some cases because they didn't have much structure at home. They seemed to love the predictability and routines once they caught on. She noticed the difference in their behavior over time because of the consistent expectations.

The loyal volunteer was sad the Club had to curtail volunteering for health reasons during the COVID pandemic. She worried about how it was affecting the children. How were they learning to read, do math, write, and socialize?

"There is more need for Boys & Girls Clubs now than ever in history," she said. "Everybody has some time to pour into someone else's life and to see how far just a little bit of attention and energy goes in changing it for the better. It makes it all worthwhile."

Having served in a law enforcement career and seen firsthand the negative impact of the lack of good role models, Suzanne mentioned how important it is for good, responsible adults to get involved as mentors and volunteers in programs like the Boys & Girls Clubs. "There are plenty of harmful people out there, making it critical for loving, kind, good role models to become part of their lives," she noted.

"It was a great honor to volunteer at the Boys & Girls Club. I wish everybody could do it."

CHAPTER 13
Bridging Boundaries

"The stories shared by Boys & Girls Club members reminded me how different life can be for someone my age… how important it is to have a place to go, a place to belong, food provided, and adults who care for you. These simple things can be taken for granted."

—Josh Linholm, fundraising co-chair

There were many milestones to celebrate while I was at the Boys & Girls Clubs, but one of the most meaningful for me personally came near the end of my time as CEO. I had the unique opportunity to introduce kids from the suburb where I live, and where my biological children grew up, to "my" kids at the Club. While all young people have potential and promise, sadly, the zip code they are born in sometimes affects the opportunities they are given. "My" Club kids attended schools in woefully over-challenged and under-resourced public-school districts, while our home district in an Oklahoma City suburb was known for its community support and academic strength. I wanted "my" kids from various zip codes to have a chance to get to know and appreciate each other, their future co-workers and neighbors.

The opportunity to connect youth across community boundaries came about by tapping into one of the suburban high school's traditions of raising money for a medical needs or local nonprofit organizations. The fundraising tradition had begun in 1986, when a small group of students started thinking beyond themselves to raise money for a child who needed a kidney transplant. They approached the principal, who supported the idea and even agreed to kiss a pig if they reached their fundraising goal. They raised $3,000 that first year, but more importantly, they started an annual tradition that created an environment of compassion and philanthropy throughout the high school for years to come.

As the fundraising goals increased and the tradition evolved, the school's student council began requiring applications for assistance. They became more intentional about gauging the anticipated student body's passion for the chosen project, to be galvanized during a special week of celebrations. The students' ability to raise money had gained momentum, and the process had gotten very competitive throughout the metropolitan area. It would be a longshot for the Boys & Girls Clubs to be chosen as the recipient of their generosity, but we believed there would be great value in helping youth from across the metropolitan area join hands for a shared purpose.

Thirty-three years after the special fundraising week's beginning, the timing for the Boys & Girls Clubs' application turned out to be perfect because it involved kids getting personally involved in creating better opportunities for their peers. The Boys & Girls Club was trying to raise $1.6 million for a 6,122-square-foot Teen Center addition to our Clubhouse, a project we hoped the suburban student body could get excited about.

Most of the kids who attended the suburban high school had parents with college degrees and professional careers. It wasn't unusual to see BMWs or Range Rovers in the school parking lot. These students' personal and family resources allowed them to focus on their studies, friendships, extracurricular activities, and plans for the future. In contrast, many of their

> There is universal agreement that a quality education is vital to helping children create productive futures and reach their potential. Young people in impoverished neighborhoods typically have few, if any, choices about where they attend school. In *Our Kids: The Crisis of the American Dream*, Robert D. Putnam points out that since the 1970s, increasing class-based residential segregation has evolved into de facto class-based school segregation. School children from the top half of income distribution increasingly attend private schools or public schools in more wealthy suburban school districts. A family's economic status and transportation capability are far greater indicators of the ability to choose a school than any other variables.

peers at the Boys & Girls Clubs were barely getting by day today, with no emotional capacity to plan for the future.

Very few teens at the Club owned their own vehicles, and most rode a Boys & Girls Club bus, school bus, or city bus to the Club after school. They had struggles that were largely unheard of by the suburban kids: nearly twenty percent were in the state's foster care system, and around thirty percent had experienced having at least one incarcerated family member. They needed the Club for many things, including a decent meal. They also relied on it to be a safe space with caring adults who could help with homework and identify solutions to personal problems.

A former Club member shared his experiences in the written application to become the chosen philanthropy: "Besides the Club being a home, it was having someone there. When I was young, my family was struggling for food. I sometimes had to take a city bus to get to school, often sitting out in the cold, but when I got to the Club, all that hurt and pain was gone. I didn't feel it anymore. The Club gave me confidence in myself and an education. It made me feel secure and safe."

There was one thing about the Club the teens didn't like, however: walking in the front doors alongside kindergartners! Our Club served youth five to eighteen years old, and for safety reasons, the Clubhouse had been built with only one entrance. Although the teens had a couple of rooms to themselves, their neighborhood friends often teased them about going to a daycare with a bunch of little kids.

Club teens had heard rumors about plans to build a separate wing to the Clubhouse that would be strictly their own. They would have their own entrance as well as a technology center, art room, music performance studio, video game room, and spacious areas to hang out with each other, mentors, and speakers. It would be first-class but expensive, and they knew that their ten-dollars-a-year membership fees couldn't make it happen.

In an effort to make their dreams come true, the Boys & Girls Club competed with over eighty nonprofits in the metropolitan area to become the 2019 fundraising week recipient. The funds raised would build a new wing especially for teens at our main Clubhouse.

The suburban students' philanthropic co-chairs, Olivia Scott, Brooke Guarry, and Josh Linholm, as well as their advisor and mentor Jeff Lovett, were impressed with the programs the Club offered in five core areas:
1. Character and leadership development
2. Educational and career development
3. Health and life skills
4. The arts
5. Sports, fitness, and recreation

While kids from families in all economic categories need opportunities in each of these areas to thrive, access for kids and teens from lower income families often is more limited. Like the uneven distribution of financial capital, the uneven distribution of social capital creates an unlevel playing field.

Students from the suburban high school had likely been able to take music, dance, sports, and/or art lessons from an early age, but most Club kids had not had those same opportunities to develop their talents in their early years. Programs in the five core areas gave kids at the Club a chance to explore their interests and skills. Especially for teens, the ability to hang out with friends in a safe and positive environment—without the influence of gangs, drugs, and sex—was also particularly important to their positive development.

The organization convinced the suburban high school students that their fundraising could make a meaningful difference by making it possible for the Boys & Girls Club to serve more teens in increasingly robust and meaningful ways. Club staff shared statistics collected annually through anonymous surveys of Club members as proof that investing in Boys & Girls Club experiences pays positive dividends:

Only four percent of Club members had reported using alcohol in the past thirty days, compared to a thirty-five percent national average.

Only five percent of Club teens reported using marijuana in the last thirty days, compared to twenty-three percent of teens nationwide.

While one hundred percent of Oklahoma County Boys & Girls Club teens expected to graduate from high school, the primary school district's average graduation rate was seventy-three percent.

Beyond statistics, however, the real catalyst for opening the program leaders' hearts came when they saw the faces of their underserved peers as they arrived on buses after school. Josh, Brooke, and Olivia told me years later that it was the first-time student council members had made site visits to help identify the organization they wanted to support and how meaningful the visit to the Club was. The student council members noticed the teens coming in the front doors of the Clubhouse surrounded by kindergartners and first graders, eager to get past the front desk and find a space where they could be together and be themselves.

> The Children of America's Defense Fund's State of America's Children 2021 Report, states that while COVID-19 crippled our country's public education system even further, America's schools were deeply segregated and inequitable long before the pandemic.
>
> Every school district in the US where segregation along racial and economic lines is high—or even moderate—has a large achievement gap.

"When we came to the Boys & Girls Club, you could just feel the love," Brooke said. "Energy feeds off other energy, and the energy there was so positive and fun as the kids ran into the Club."

ACTIVITIES RAMP UP

All told, the philanthropic fundraising "week" was more like a seven-month experience considering the grantee selection process and preparations for upcoming events. The first official event was in January when the student council members and Royalty (school students committed to raising funds) came to the Memorial Park Club for an appreciation dinner and to meet some of the teens they would be helping.

They enjoyed playing basketball, listening to music, and getting acquainted with each other, although the student council kids felt a deep void because a member of their leadership team couldn't be with them. A heart attack had taken the life of Brooke's father just the week before, but that one event was the only activity she missed. Her dedication, commitment, and inner strength to continue to perform her leadership responsibilities inspired all. Even in the depths of the family's dire grief, she was an outstanding leader, and her twin sister and mom also remained engaged throughout.

The next week, a Boys & Girls Clubs staff leader escorted a group of eight-year-old girls from the Club to enjoy a school-hosted Daddy Daughter Dance, followed by a giant auction attended by hundreds of people from the community.

The suburban teens were soon back at the Boys & Girls Club to challenge Club teens in a dodgeball tournament. Afterwards, they worked together to paint walls and room signs around the Clubhouse. Other events attended by several Boys & Girls Clubs' members, staff, and board members included a run/walk through downtown, a bowling tournament, a haunted house, a dog show at the high school, a basketball tournament at a middle school, a golf tournament, a spirit/cheerleading clinic, and sales of T-shirts and sweatshirts with original designs. All of these creative, inclusive, and fun events required significant planning and implementation by students and faculty, and resulted in tremendous community-building and support for the project and for the organization.

A WEEK LIKE NONE OTHER!

The myriad of activities not only raised money but also built growing anticipation for the actual event week, just prior to spring break. The theme of the week was Dr. Sooie, a fun mash-up with Dr. Suess books and the principal's pledge to kiss a pig. Students packed the high school the weekend prior, painting nearly every inch of the hallway walls with images of Dr. Suess characters and quotes. Dr. Suess messages painted on walls throughout the school were teeming with inspiration, such as: "To the world you may be one person, but to one person you may be the world."

One Senior was quoted in the school newspaper saying, "The decorations every year just show how much we care. This year there were a lot more students engaging, which I felt really embodied the purpose… to work together to show how much we care about the organization."

The high school hosted an assembly for its two thousand students each day of the special week. The freshman, sophomore, junior, and senior classes sat in their own sections in the bleachers of the large basketball gymnasium. Many of the activities during the week pitted classes against each other to create friendly competition for raising money. Buckets to collect cash were passed around at the end of each assembly. Day One kicked off with a bang, literally, with members of Royalty shooting off confetti cannons into the crowd. Representatives from the Boys & Girls Clubs shared stories about Club members and the need to expand and enhance opportunities with the Teen Center.

Anthony, a Boys & Girls Club teen, sang "The Star-Spangled Banner" during the second day assembly and immediately became a school favorite. He taught the student body a fun musical swag-surfing activity that the students repeated at each following assembly. Brooke told me four years later that school assemblies still to this day include Anthony's swag-surfing song.

Jennifer Lickteig shared her personal story of how being part of a Club in California changed her life after she got in serious trouble with the law. Like many local Club kids, her story included food insecurity, sexual abuse, and lack of positive role models before she was ordered to provide community service at the California Club. She pointed to each separate class section at the assembly and described what life was like for her as a freshman, sophomore, junior, and senior. Then, she shocked the audience by challenging them with a dollar-for-dollar match if the students could meet their daily fundraising goal. Deafening applause and cheers erupted throughout the gymnasium.

FINAL ASSEMBLY ANNOUNCED OVERALL TOTAL RAISED: $587,592!

A moment of complete silence fell over the entire gymnasium before an eruption of thunderous cheering, clapping, laughing, and joyful tears as organizers revealed the final fundraising number! It was the highest amount raised by students in that high school's history…a far cry from their $3,000 raised their first philanthropic venture. Well over half a million dollars took the Boys & Girls Club Teen Center funding over the top, assuring that it would be built and fully equipped.

Fundraising co-chairs Brooke, Olivia, and Josh with board member Jennifer Lickteig

The grand total!

Boys & Girls Club kindergartners through seniors came on Club buses to attend the final assembly and were overwhelmed by the love demonstrated by their new friends. Bridging the boundaries provided meaning and purpose for the suburban students as well.

TEENS HELPING TEENS

The three amazing fundraising co-chairs, Olivia, Brooke, and Josh, were beyond their years in creativity, maturity, compassion, and the ability to provide meaningful opportunities for their peers at the Club. I wanted to reconnect with them years later to catch up on their lives and ask them to share any lessons learned from the experience. Brooke had just returned from a mission trip in India and Thailand, and Olivia had plans to leave for the Grand Canyon later that week, but they took time to get together for brunch at my house one July morning.

After visiting about what was going on in their lives, I asked them to reminisce about their efforts to raise money for the Teen Center at the Boys & Girls Club and to share any insights they might have. They expressed gratitude for their student council sponsor and mentor, Mr. Lovett, as well as the Boys & Girls Clubs administrative staff who also mentored them along the way.

Olivia mentioned the impact the project made on their fellow classmates by saying, "The teen years are so pivotal for self-confidence and knowing who you are. From our school's students' perspective, learning to serve others at such a young age was important. We were changed as well." She added that the entire student body learned that any amount you can contribute can make a difference, which was a valuable life lesson. No one donation was big enough to meet the need, yet many small gifts combined to exceed the goal. While the next year's philanthropic event at the school raised a slightly higher total, the three co-chairs said they were proud that their total gift was a result of broader participation rather than one large donor.

"Learning how to give is so important," Brooke said. "We learned through planning and raising money that it is so much greater to serve. Our school's students were excited because they knew we were making a difference for other kids. It was something bigger than ourselves. We wanted to be co-chairs to take on that huge task and make a big difference, with the spotlight on the organization."

Olivia said that, as a recent college graduate, she just recently came to realize how easy it is—especially when you are financially secure—to focus on and care most about status. She followed that observation by saying, "It doesn't matter how much we have, it's more about how we treat people and show love. Serving others is so much more fulfilling than a certain status. All kids deserve to thrive!"

Brooke talked about how the Club exposes kids to more satisfying ways to live and that she could see that Club members were actively working hard because they wanted better futures. She mentioned being inspired by the board member's story about her California Club experience and how she matched student contributions for the day. Jenn's story showed her that Club kids not only can break their own cycle of poverty but that they often choose to give back.

Olivia said she went back to visit after the Teen Center was completed and "saw that the kids felt like they had a home there…that they could dream from that safe space. They could be seen, heard, and understood." She compared those feelings to how she and her other co-chairs felt as part of their student council.

Josh added that when he visited the Teen Center addition it "didn't feel like an after-school program. It just felt like a place the kids wanted to be. They seemed to feel valued and had a sense of community."

When I asked them what the hardest part of the process was for them, they said it was easy to get your self-worth tied into meeting the invisible standard, and they worried about raising enough money. "Pride can take over your heart," Brooke said. Olivia added that there was pressure to be the best experience ever—no bad events, more money raised than ever before.

After high school graduation, Brooke served as an intern at ReMerge, a pre-trial diversion program in Oklahoma City that serves high-risk, high-needs mothers facing non-violent felony offenses. She said that experience made her even more aware of how difficult it is to break the cycle of multigenerational poverty, making the work of organizations like Boys & Girls Clubs even more relevant and vital. Many of the high school students came to the grand opening of the Teen Center and were able to see firsthand the site where they helped create better futures for thousands of kids who would become their future co-workers and neighbors.

CHAPTER 14
Many Ways to Mentor

"At the end of the day, it's not about what you have or even what you've accomplished… it's about who you've lifted up, who you've made better. It's about what you've given back."

—Denzel Washington, *Hand to Guide Me*

This book has barely scratched the surface of the obstacles facing our country's youth and the difference researched-based programs and caring mentors can make. Having time in retirement to reconnect with a few young people, staff, and volunteers I had gotten to know at the Boys & Girls Clubs of Oklahoma County provides hope, however. It solidified my belief that just a little intervention in the life of a child can make a tremendous, lasting, legacy-shaping difference. Example after example demonstrates that safe environments, caring adults, and the opportunity to try new things can open promising pathways to help youth in our country build better futures, resulting in stronger communities.

I believe they are ALL our kids, and that it is up to us to try our best to provide the resources for each of them to reach their potential. While every human life will be challenged by obstacles and disappointments, millions of kids in our country are faced with the need to overcome extraordinary trauma due to no fault of their own.

The Hope Research Center in Oklahoma focuses on the relationship between the power of hope and the ability to overcome trauma to thrive. Founding Director Dr. Chan Hellman's recent presentation at a local Rotary Club reminded me that a common denominator in the success stories told by former Boys & Girls Club kids is that they were each given the encouragement *and* the pathways to realistically hope for a better future, despite their challenged beginnings. Dr. Hellman said the desire with no pathway is just a wish and that the opposite of hope is apathy.

The Arizona State Center for the Advanced Study and Practice of Hope provides what they have determined are three universal truths:
1. Every child—no exceptions—is capable of success.
2. Connection between adults and youth is meaningful and impactful.
3. Goal setting happens in many areas, including education and career, home and family, community and service, and hobbies and recreation.

It is clear to me that Boys & Girls Clubs across the country provide the safe and nurturing environment through which kids find hope and not only identify and establish goals but, with the help of staff and volunteer mentors, find the pathways to achieve them. Caring adults are there to provide programs and resources that present new opportunities and to spot and knock down obstacles that would otherwise derail a child's progress. In contrast, millions of kids in our country have the desire to grow and succeed, but face so many obstacles blocking their paths that they lose hope and become apathetic.

While it is impossible to know what the outcomes would have been for the kids whose stories are in this book without their Boys & Girls Club experiences, I believe that it's likely that some may not have lived to adulthood. Without a doubt, fewer, if any, would be first generation college graduates. And, particularly tragic, without their involvement at the Boys & Girls Club, the impact of their childhood trauma would have become their legacies to pass on to future generations. Instead, they found hope and help identifying realistic pathways for envisioning and achieving their dreams, changing the trajectory of their lives and the lives of generations to follow.

Hope for America's Youth: Beyond the Blue Doors of a Boys & Girls Club highlights a proven model for transformative change that occurs every day at Boys & Girls Clubs throughout the country. This book offers real-life examples of Club members, staff, mentors, and communities who have been made stronger through their purposeful associations with one another.

One of the most distinctive and powerful aspects of Boys & Girls Clubs is that they provide **_long-term positive relationships_** that schools and other organizations can't provide. Having a front-row seat to watch many young people grow from kindergarteners to high school seniors was such a gift. It was a joy to reconnect with A.Jaye, LaRissa, and Sharon, who represent the dedicated staff everywhere who create those long-term mentor relationships and opportunities.

I have become even more convinced that **_multigenerational transformations_** are possible when youth who have suffered poverty and/or abuse are encouraged to recognize their talents and strengths to create better opportunities for themselves and the next generation. I marvel at Jessica's loving and dedicated approach to parenting, educating her own children, and advocating on behalf of young children everywhere.

I was reminded how **_multicultural environments_** celebrate the differences of youth from various ethnicities and cultures and enrich the lives of individuals, families, and communities. Sergio, AnaMarie, and Adan's family histories began in other countries, yet their stories demonstrate that the language of love needs no interpreter and transcends national boundaries. They each credit their Boys & Girls Clubs experiences and long-term mentor relationships for helping them discover their potential and pathways to success. The benefits to them and their descendants will continue to expand, making our community richer with diversity and understanding.

I heard example after example of the difference that just **_listening_**, really listening, can make, and I am grateful for Veronica providing listening ears and pathways of hope for families struggling with addiction. I am certain that Leo will help others celebrate life by listening to what makes their hearts sing. And, although her struggles are still formidable, I'm grateful Mary Kate has felt heard and loved.

I deepened my gratitude for **_boomerang Club alums_**, who come back around as adults to serve others, whether as staff members, board members, or financial donors, leaving ongoing legacies as part of the Boys & Girls Club family business. It will continue to bring me joy to watch the difference Rick, Jennifer, and Carl make through their investments in young lives.

I celebrated the stunning difference that ***volunteer mentors*** make by revisiting the stories of Cliff, Donna, Wes, and Suzanne and how their involvement has impacted them personally as well as the young people they've mentored along the way.

I found joy in remembering how the lives of ***multi-community youth*** from my hometown were enriched by getting to know "my" kids at the Boys & Girls Club, learning to understand, appreciate, and build connections with their peers. I was inspired by reconnecting with Josh, Brooke, and Olivia and hearing about their continued commitment to building relationships across cultural, ethnic, and socioeconomic invisible boundaries.

Boys & Girls Clubs exist in nearly every community, and I am convinced now more than ever that if you will get involved in one, it will enrich your life. It certainly has mine. Not everyone can be a professional staff member at a Club, but there are many ways to serve. Angels come in all forms, and some come with a checkbook in hand.

It is important to recognize that Boys & Girls Clubs simply would not exist without the financial support and leadership provided by multiple people, businesses, and organizations in their communities. Just a few local examples from my personal experience include

- the hundreds of dedicated people who have served on the organization's board of directors over the years, spending countless hours studying materials, planning and attending events, volunteering at the Club, encouraging staff, and providing the strong governance and leadership that make everything else possible;
- the woman who wrote a $100,000 check after touring the Club for the first time when she saw how happy the kids were despite traumatic situations some of them faced, reminding her of her own difficult childhood;
- the attendee at the organization's annual gala who was so moved by the stories shared there that she pledged to provide scholarship money for each Youth of the Year for a decade;

- the individuals and organizations, including teenagers, who stepped up financially to build a new Teen Center addition to the Club;
- the woman from Oklahoma City Community Foundation who appeared in my office early the morning after the Clubhouse flooded to offer immediate and substantial financial assistance;
- volunteers from the United Way of Central Oklahoma who toured the Club and scrutinized the organization's governance and financial statements each year to validate that we were performing as a credible and trustworthy United Way partner agency;
- the couple who learned that the Club had a significant and urgent need for transportation vehicles and casually offered on the spot to pay for two thirty-four-passenger buses;
- the tall, distinguished community philanthropist who kindly knelt to tie the shoelaces of a kindergartener during his first visit after investing generously in the Club's construction;
- leaders of philanthropic foundations and organizations who offered sage advice and encouragement in addition to recurring generous financial support;
- the hand-delivered $400,000 check from the Chickasaw Nation to pay off the Club's building mortgage debt;
- the phone call from a gentleman asking how he could transfer stock to the Club, and when asked the approximate amount to be donated, said with all humility, "around a million dollars;" and
- city leaders who listened, observed, and celebrated the difference Boys & Girls Clubs can make for families and the community, and supported inclusion of four Youth Centers as part of a giant sales tax effort to improve the city.

OTHER WAYS TO MAKE A DIFFERENCE

While I believe that the evidenced-based programing, attention to safety, staff training, organizational fiscal requirements, the single focus on youth out-of-school time, and multi-year relationships equip Boys & Girls Clubs to serve the largest number of youth with the strongest impact, I recognize there are many ways to help children and teens create positive pathways to success. Depending on your community and your personal interest and availability, below are a few stories from other organizations making a positive impact.

Court Appointed Special Advocates (CASA) around the country provide vetted and trained volunteers to be champions for children who have been removed from their home due to abuse or neglect. They get to know the children and communicate with all parties and people in the child's life to provide sound recommendations to the court. As "the eyes and ears" of the judge, the CASA volunteer offers a neutral, third-party opinion to the court, one that is child-focused.

After retiring from twenty-four years as a middle school and high school English/fine arts teacher, Cindy Birdwell worked in about twenty cases as a CASA volunteer in Oklahoma over the course of a decade. She was inspired to get involved with CASA after remembering some of her former students telling her they would be absent from school the next day because they had to go to court. She said the kids always seemed confused and scared, and she would think to herself, "I wish I could go with you."

Her first case involved a teenager named Henry, who was removed from his home following sexual abuse of his sister. He was not directly involved in the abuse, but the court decided that his mother's mental illness and lack of oversight made the home unsafe. Cindy said Henry was confused and angry about being sent to foster care. He continually told her, "I don't belong in foster care. I'm going to rise above it." She said his defiance about the situation created an internal resilience that served him well.

With his persistence, resilience, and Cindy's support, he did "rise above it," graduating from college and later becoming a world traveler.

She laughed when she told me a story about Henry's very first plane trip. He had gotten tickets to fly from Oklahoma City to Australia to visit his aunt and uncle after graduating from college. She had warned him about what a long trip it would be and gave him hints about ways to pass the time while in flight. She was surprised and amused by his call after he arrived at the Dallas airport a short time later when he told her, "It didn't take so long!" He naively thought that he had arrived in Australia. She said that story reminds her of the narrow worldviews many kids have due to their limited exposure. Henry told Cindy years later that when he first met her, he thought she was "just another white woman here to ruin my life." She said despite his dubious first impression, they "clicked" over time, and that he is now a self-sufficient twenty-eight-year-old who remains in touch with his former CASA worker.

The children in several of Cindy's cases were able to attend the Boys & Girls Club after school and during school breaks. When I asked her how that impacted their outcomes, she was quick to respond: "It was fabulous when 'my' kids could go to the Boys & Girls Club! I could take a deep breath that they weren't home alone after school. I could take a deep breath they were not on the street. I could take a deep breath that they were getting tutoring help. I could take a deep breath that they were part of a positive community."

CASA began in 1977 when the number of children in foster care in the country reached nearly a half a million. Judge David Soukup, a Seattle Court judge, found himself losing sleep over the number of children entering foster care. He knew his daily decisions forever changed the lives of abused and neglected children and wanted to improve his ability to make informed choices for the youth. Over time, judges around the nation saw the value and impact and began CASA programs in their local communities. At this writing, there are more than nine hundred CASA programs in forty-nine states.

Sports leagues within and outside of school athletics can provide mentors, structure, exercise, and sportsmanship lessons for kids even in the toughest neighborhoods. A local organization, **Fields and Futures**, has invested millions of dollars in creating first-rate football, soccer, baseball, track, and other fields in low-income neighborhoods all over town. They have worked with the Police Athletic League and an army of volunteers to help youth in our community with documented success.

Dot Rhyne, executive director of Fields and Futures, shared the story of Jeremie, an example of one young person significantly impacted by their work in our community. When he was in seventh grade, Jeremie had twenty-eight suspensions that kept him out of class for one hundred days.

"I was in class, and a kid got up and started yelling and shook his desk at me," he said. "I thought, 'I'm not gonna let him do this,' so I picked the desk up and hit him with it. I was a troubled kid. When my grandma died, she was like my second mom, and when she died, our whole family split apart. I didn't know how to react, and I started being bad.

"I was really angry and upset. Sports is what had helped me, but when I got suspended, I couldn't play football and had no place to put my anger. So, my coach sat me down in the office and said, 'Son, it's like this. When you get out of high school, there will be no suspensions. You're going to get one year, two years, or whatever in prison. Adults don't get suspensions.' That got my attention.

"We used to play on dirt. Nothing but dirt and broken beer bottles. But when I went back to school the next year, there was a whole new grass field. No dirt or beer bottles, just nice grass. It changes you emotionally. When they [Fields and Futures] did that project, it changed me, and I am very thankful for that."

Jeremie finished his high school career with over a four-point grade average and has since graduated from college and started a family.

For over twenty-five years, **Kids Hope USA** has provided a proven mentorship program through church partnerships with schools. They train and equip volunteers to reach kids in public schools who would benefit from additional caring, reliable, one-on-one relationships. Mentors, standing alongside teachers and parents, show kids that they are not alone. Through the power of relationships, struggling students can build resilience and brighter futures.

Many Ways to Mentor

What started as a one-year commitment to the Kids Hope program for Cathy and Don Gilmore turned out to be a decade-long relationship between the couple and a family of four kids crying out for help. It began several years ago when Don agreed to be a weekly mentor to kindergartner Sammy. One week, Don couldn't be there, so he asked his wife, Cathy, to substitute for him. She enjoyed that experience, so the following year, Cathy began working with Sammy's little sister Brandi. They continued to meet weekly with both kids through fifth grade and stayed in touch afterwards.

Seven years after Sammy and Brandi left elementary school, their mom reached out to see if the church was still doing the Kids Hope program and asked if she could get mentors for her two younger children, Bobby and Julie, whose father had recently ended his own life. Cathy said it was an interesting coincidence because one of the church ministers had just asked if she and Don would like to be mentors again, and although she had said probably not, when the request came to help that same sweet family, they couldn't say no.

She said the kids seem to crave their attention. Cathy and Don get invited to Grandparents Day at the school and their mom texts photos from time to time, showing the important part they play in their lives. The couple's support of that family has extended over fourteen years, and they continue to leave a legacy.

Local schools and foundations offer many volunteer opportunities. Reading Buddies is a program organized by the Oklahoma City Public School Foundation to match volunteer readers with kids who need encouragement. For an hour each week during the school year, each Reading Buddy reads together with a small group of kids. It is as much about companionship and support as it is about inspiring a love of reading (although that is a tremendous gift in itself).

I had the privilege of reading with Alexander and Angel for two years when they were in third and fourth grades. Since we started during the COVID pandemic, our times together were online via Google Meets, but we were able to read together in person the last few months. At the end of the first school year, Angel said, "Ms. Jane, we don't have anything to do on Tuesdays in the summer. Can we still read?" Google Meets made that possible, so of course, we did.

We had many wonderful moments together, but one of the times that touched me deeply was when I got teary-eyed after reading that the dog in the story had died. Angel very kindly and maturely reassured me that the book we were reading was fiction. For the past two years, I have been in a book club with a group of middle school girls, and we enjoy discussing young adult novels in various genres (between fits of laughter and occasional tears).

The foundation offers additional volunteer opportunities and encourages literacy with ReadOKC on the Go!, two converted school buses that provide new books for children throughout the community. They also sponsor Little Libraries in front of each public-school building, offering free reading materials for children and adults alike. If your school or the supporting foundation has similar programs, they can provide easy ways to get involved and have some fun.

Big Brothers Big Sisters (BBBS) is a national organization that pairs one child or teen with one mentor. It involves a commitment for the adult to spend one-on-one time with his or her little brother or sister a few hours each week. This type of program offers flexibility, including home visits, field trips, etc. The approval process to become a mentor in BBBS is appropriately extensive because it involves relationship building outside a structured group environment, but it can create lifetime relationships that can make a tremendous difference. BBBS.org provides the following example.

"My Big Brother Mark helped me redirect the sadness that I had after the loss of my dad. Mark turned the light back on in my heart."

Little Brother Eric was just seven years old when his father passed away. His aunt reached out to Big Brothers Big Sisters, hoping that a mentor would be someone Eric could open up to and trust, and they found that in Mark, who works in community affairs at a local bank.

In fifth grade, Eric invited Mark to his school for "Take Your Father to School Day," and when his classmates questioned Eric and Mark's connection to one another since they weren't the same race, Eric simply replied, "He's my Big Brother."

The conversations surrounding race aren't as simple when you're in high school.

In 2020, during Eric's junior year, in addition to the normal stressors of classwork, Eric was coping with the pandemic, family members who died from COVID-19, the challenges of social distancing, and the racial unrest across the country. In fact, Eric witnessed several racial incidents at his school. Mark was there to listen, sometimes not knowing exactly what to say but to offer support as an ally, attending forums and meetings surrounding the difficult conversations about racism.

What Eric appreciated the most is that Mark never pretended to understand the struggles Eric faced as a young Black man but was there to learn and grow, too. "Eric has become a young leader in the fight for racial justice," said Mark. "I look up to him in more ways than I ever thought I would."

When Eric heads to college, he'll play football, but his ultimate goal is to become a math teacher. He'll have more than basic math facts to share with his students.

Youth Leadership programs are always looking for volunteers as speakers, mentors, and transportation providers.

Boy Scouts, Girl Scouts, and Camp Fire welcome vetted volunteers in their programs throughout the country.

Churches offer Sunday School classes and summer activities, all of which usually rely heavily on adult volunteers.

YOUR LEGACY

As you take a moment to reflect on specific ways you can provide hope for kids in your community, leaving your legacy as a compassionate catalyst for change, here are a few thoughts to consider:
- It is important to share a sense of hope with young people from all walks of life, not just those in our immediate families. If we want our communities and country to remain strong, it is important to recognize and advance the God-given potential of all children. Our country's future depends on them.

- Refuse to let racial, sexual, economic, religious, or other prejudices create barriers to your being an agent for positive change in a child's life.
- Public education is the foundation for an educated and productive citizenry, but it is woefully lacking in many parts of our country. Fight for equity in education and access to opportunity. Invest your time and resources to support students in public schools.
- Focus on the mental health of youth in your various areas of influence and provide resources and opportunities for wellness.
- Find small and large ways to become part of a child's story.
- Visit your local Boys & Girls Club to see how you can get involved.

The handwritten note that accompanied flowers from Joy Reed Belt on my first day at the Boys & Girls Club predicted that I would make a difference. This book represents my continued dedication to that elusive goal. Thank you for joining me on the journey.

PERSONAL EPILOGUE

The stories in this book have highlighted youth and their mentors whose lives have been changed for the better by their associations with one another. I have been blessed by many mentors in my life, and it would feel incomplete to conclude this book without remembering three people whose direction was most instrumental in molding my heart and path as a mentor.

AN EXEMPLARY FATHER

Growing up in a small town during the 1950s with two loving parents and a strong public education system gave me the foundation for creating a rewarding life with meaningful work. The first person who taught me how relationships can build up individuals and communities was my dad, Benjamin Louis Edwards.

My father was the Ben in the Bert & Ben's Conoco Service Station in Ponca City, Oklahoma, and was one of the most hard-working and loving human beings ever to walk this Earth. He graduated with a marketing degree from Oklahoma State University in 1932. In that decade, a series of severe dust storms—the Dust Bowl—swept across the Great Plains. The storms, years of drought, and the Great Depression devastated the lives of residents in that region, including Oklahoma, and three-hundred thousand of them reportedly packed up their belongings and moved to California, including my dad. (This was the mass migration dramatized in John Steinbeck's *The Grapes of Wrath*.) Ben found work with his uncle, who had traded property in Wichita for a service station equipment company. Although he had a college degree, he worked for thirty cents an hour, digging tank holes and helping install industrial equipment. He ruptured a disc in his back doing this work, which laid him up for a couple of months and ultimately resulted in his return to Ponca City.

Ben's cousin Bert saw that motor vehicles and the booming oil business in Oklahoma spelled opportunity, so he convinced Dad to start a new gasoline service station with him. They each borrowed $2,000 and started building what later would become a town icon. They did most of the lumber work, bricking, and roofing themselves. In fact, Dad first remembered seeing his future wife (my mom, Mary Louise Oates Edwards) while putting up a roof on the station. He couldn't get "that cute young girl next door" out his head, and they would go on to marry in 1936.

Bert & Ben's Conoco Service Station opened October 7, 1934.

Younger readers may not be familiar with full-service gasoline stations. Starting in the 1980s, self-service stations took over in most states. When you drove into a full-service station, multiple servicemen scurried to your car, filled up your gas tank, checked your motor oil, measured the air in your tires, and washed your windshield. And all that for 29 cents per gallon!

Bert & Ben's Service Station

At Bert & Ben's, there was also a man named Ben, who cared more about your personal well-being than he did your car or his business. Payment was on the honor system, as my mom sent out statements to regular customers at the end of each month. For forty-seven years,

Dad worked from 6:00 a.m. to 8:00 p.m., six days a week. His skin was leathered from hours in the sun. His hands and fingernails were permanently stained black, and the smell of oil and gasoline permeated his overalls and bulky work boots.

When the weather brought snow or freezing rain, he labored late into the night, helping customers whose cars had gotten stuck or damaged. He came home with frozen limbs and an aching back that was a perpetual reminder of that ruptured disc.

Even as he got older, he worked fourteen-hour days in all harsh varieties of Oklahoma weather, taking only a short forty-five-minute break in the middle of the day to go home for lunch and a twenty-minute catnap. The audible tick-tick-tick of the white and black kitchen timer on the dresser counted down brief moments of rest.

Often to the irritation of my older sister and me, Dad lined up playdates for us when his customers had grandchildren in town, or he sometimes asked our mom to bake an angel food cake for someone who had just had surgery. Bert & Ben's was a community hub.

Dad was ahead of his time in embracing and supporting people of different ethnicities and genders, although he grew up in a society of racial segregation and strict gender roles. He was quick to offer fatherly advice and cash, loans, or gifts when the young men who worked at the station faced hard times. They respected and trusted him, and he was a stabilizing influence in their lives.

As a child of the 1960s, I tested his acceptance of the women's liberation movement by pressing for the opportunity to work at the station during summer break, just like my two older brothers had done. He not only allowed me, a teenage girl, to work with him but ordered top-of-the-line Conoco green coveralls with embroidered Bert & Ben's red letters on the back and "Janie" over the front pocket.

Despite looking "coveralls cool," it turned, out I was not cut out to be a gas station service technician! At five foot two, I could not even reach the middle of the windshields of those giant 1960's sedans, and I honestly didn't care too much for gasoline or motor oil on my hands. He never said a word about it after I went home for lunch never to return as an employee. Although I didn't make it through a full day working at the station, my dad's work ethic and example had profound effects on me. They guided me through my first summer job at the *Ponca City News*, a thirty-year career with local governments at the Association of Central Oklahoma Governments, and then finally, the Boys & Girls Clubs of Oklahoma County.

Citizens elected Ben to serve on the Ponca City Board of Education. He was a faithful member of the Rotary Club with many years of perfect attendance (including finding Rotary meetings when we were out of town on vacation). One of his favorite activities was distributing plaques to area schools that displayed the text of the Rotary Four-Way Test: Is it the truth? Will it build goodwill and friendships? Is it fair to all? Will it be beneficial to all concerned? He lived by those questions, and they have guided me through my life and career as well. He also regularly volunteered for the United Way, raising money for important services for those struggling in town. Belief in the value of the United Way also followed me into adulthood as a leader of ACOG's United Way drives, then ultimately as a CEO of a United Way partner agency.

While society may not view owning a gasoline service station as a significant career accomplishment, I had a front-row seat to watch how my father used his place on that concrete drive to do impactful work and create a life of purpose. He built a more welcoming and compassionate community because he understood that the real meaning of full-service was caring for people.

A PURPOSEFUL BOSS

Just as my dad had experienced, I graduated from college in a challenging economic climate in the mid-1970s. I was grateful to stumble on to a worthy yet rather complicated government agency. ACOG helps cities, towns, and counties collectively envision a better future for their citizens.

In my thirty-year career there, under the direction of Executive Director Zach D. Taylor, the board of directors and staff accomplished many things of significance for the community. Among the most noteworthy and recognizable achievements were the creation of the region's first enhanced 9-1-1 system, protection of the Garber-Wellington Aquifer that supplied a third of the area's drinking water, plans for the metropolitan area's street and highway system, and attention to environmental concerns like air quality.

Zach was not just my boss but an unparalleled mentor and role model. He modeled servant leadership that was informed, strategic, and built on solid relationships of trust. Working with him for twenty-eight years taught me the tools I would need to later lead an essential and growing nonprofit.

We first met at Westminster Presbyterian Church in 1979, soon after my husband, David, and I moved to Oklahoma City. David worked with Zach's wife, Alison, at Liberty Bank and waved at her from across the sanctuary when he caught her eye after a Sunday morning service. I asked Zach about his work and found his knowledgeable description of ACOG quite intriguing.

Growing up in a small town, I had not heard of councils of government and had no awareness or appreciation of the roles they played, particularly in a metropolitan area like Central Oklahoma. It was interesting to imagine the complexities involved in governance at that level. I was working in the advertising department of the Economy Company Publishing Company at the time, but when I saw a classified advertisement in the *Daily Oklahoman* regarding a public communications position at ACOG, I remembered that conversation with Zach and decided to apply.

It was not an easy the job to get, however. Starting with an in-depth interview with Zach and deputy directors Odell Morgan and Jeff Spelman, they introduced me to a world of behind-the-scenes governance. I wore a brown tweed suit, striped shirt, and brown heels, trying to impress, but instead, they impressed me with their knowledge and passion for their work. They talked about meeting the needs of the larger community and the challenges of getting local leaders from different locations to recognize and work together on shared goals.

Investing in people and leading with heart: Zach taught me a tremendous amount about local, state, and federal governments, but most importantly, about leadership, the art of building relationships, and collaborative visioning to expand the potential of a community. A consummate relationship builder, he knew the importance of trust and the value of bringing together people from different backgrounds and perspectives to work toward the common good. He cared as much about the diminutive woman who cleaned our offices at the end of the day as he did any mayor, state legislator, or US senator.

Zach was only thirty-two years old when he became the executive director of the organization in a very tumultuous period. The suburban communities and counties were at odds with the central city. The regional organization had become dysfunctional, and the previous director was told to pack his bags.

Although the federal government required cities to work together on transportation issues for street and highway dollars, issues of control and lack of communication brought progress to a halt. Through masterful communication and strategy, Zach led the elected leadership of mayors, councilmembers, and county commissioners through a process to create a voting structure that all considered fair (and still used today). It accounted for population size, but also provided assurances that a certain number of entities must approve a decision. It protected the smaller cities from control by the central city, and the largest city from being bamboozled by the suburbs and counties.

When I joined the team just a couple of years later, under his leadership and this new voting structure, its member cities, towns, and counties were working in concert to create shared visions for the region's future.

Inspiring Mentorship: Zach's leadership went beyond the business of ACOG. While always keeping his eye on the bigger vision, he had a heart for investing in individuals within his sphere of influence. Thankfully, that included me. Zach's mentorship opened many doors and unlocked my potential for the later opportunity of a lifetime. He encouraged me to apply to join Leadership Oklahoma City Class X, assuring me that the relationships built through that process would help me accomplish both my professional and personal goals.

Zach passed away unexpectedly in 2008, and after his death, Leadership Oklahoma City created the Zach D. Taylor Servant Leadership Award.

They presented the initial honor to his wife Alison, and daughters Elizabeth and Lauren, to recognize his exemplary service to the organization. It continues to honor others who have shown similar servant leadership characteristics. Receiving the Zach D. Taylor Servant Leadership Award in 2014 was one of my most satisfying accomplishments. I continue to enjoy remembering and honoring Zach each year as we recognize others for their servant leadership. His legacy of community commitment lives on through the lives and actions of many others.

A CHILD LEADS THE WAY

In 1995, a beautiful, bright-eyed eight-year-old named Alecia found her way into my heart, foreshadowing my ultimate career purpose.

The local chamber of commerce and the public-school foundation recruited business leaders to volunteer in our urban public schools. They saw a need for positive role models who would show the children that the community cared. Our office answered the call with a group of twenty-five employees to volunteer on a weekly basis. The first stop was a local elementary school surrounded by eight-foot-high metal fences along a state highway. Broken-down cars and trucks lined the neighborhood streets, a visual metaphor for the obstacles the families faced. Our team became mystery pen-pals with an entire third-grade class. Twenty-five sets of eyes stared me down when I walked into the classroom each week to deliver and pick up the mail. Sitting at the small desk next to the window was my pen-pal Alecia. Drawings of colorful flowers and happy faces decorated her wide-ruled notebook paper stationery. She wrote about her hopes and dreams as well as her longing to meet me, her mystery correspondent.

At the end of the school year, we staged a party at our offices and asked each of the kids to send ahead an item of clothing, hair barrette, toy, or anything they could use to identify their adult pal at the party. Alecia quickly spotted her pink and purple hair scrunchy wrapped around my wrist. The balloons, towering stacks of pizza boxes, decorative cookies, and shrieks of happiness when the pen-pals found each other for the first time filled the conference room with joy and hope!

Alecia lived with her mom and younger sister in an apartment with few amenities. Thankfully, over time, her mom grew to trust me and allowed both girls to spend time with our family.

Alecia and her sister especially loved playing hide-and-go-seek after nightfall when our house was dark. You could hear their giggles throughout the upstairs bedrooms, but their unique "always keep moving" version of hide-and-seek made it nearly impossible to catch them. When they experienced the joy of eating fresh red and green grapes for the first time, they could not get enough of those cold bits of healthy wonder on a hot summer's day.

Our lifeguard son taught them to swim and later taught Alecia how to water-ski as a special treat on her tenth birthday. She told me years later, however, that the best thing she learned from our time together was a love for reading, a passion and skill that catapulted her into successful adulthood instead of generational poverty.

Alecia's family moved frequently, making it difficult to stay in touch. Although she had attended seventeen schools by the time she got to high school, her intelligence and dedication allowed her to keep her grades up and remain in a state program called Oklahoma's Promise that covered tuition for state-run colleges and universities. She traveled with me to Oklahoma State University (OSU), where we visited with the head of the African American Studies department, who was interested in mentoring first-generation college students like Alecia. He offered additional scholarships to cover her room, board, and textbooks. She was interested in studying nutrition, and a highlight of the day was meeting a doctoral level nutrition student who had come from a similar family background. Alecia seemed excited about becoming a collegiate Cowboy, and we spent the day imagining a bright academic future.

With her mom's urging and a change of direction, Alecia ended up joining the Marines, putting a pause on her academic plans. After an honorable discharge from the Marines, however, she rose above her challenging circumstances to put herself through school at Wesleyan College in Bartlesville, Oklahoma. She worked full-time and attended classes at night to earn her bachelor's degree.

And, she didn't stop there. Alecia recently earned a Master's in Business Administration degree (MBA) and was selected to be the student commencement speaker for her 2023 graduating class in Phoenix, Arizona. Prior to graduation, she texted the following message to me: "I will be graduating with my MBA from Grand Canyon University in October because God placed people like you in my life so long ago." Of course, this touched me deeply, but I doubt Alecia can even imagine the role she played in shaping *my* life.

I believe that sweet, intelligent, and inquisitive little girl prepared my heart for the last season of my career. A framed photograph on my ACOG desk of eight-year-old Alecia traveled with me to the desk at the Boys & Girls Club as a constant reminder of the difference a little intervention can make.

With gratitude for how Ben, Zach, and Alecia created legacies in me that led to meaningful work in the twilight of my career, this book was written to celebrate mentors who leave legacies in others. You are creating constellations of hope by helping children reach for the stars.

REFERENCES

America's Health Rankings. "Teen Suicide in United States." Accessed April 10, 2024. www.americashealthrankings.org/explore/health-of-women-and-children/measure/teen_suicide/state/ALL.

Barker, Joel A. *Paradigms: The Business of Discovering the Future.* New York: Harper Collins, 1993.

Boys & Girls Clubs of America. Accessed April 10, 2024. www.bgca.org.

Bradshaw, John. *Healing the Shame That Binds You.* New York: Simon & Schuster, 2010.

Cox, John, and Steven Rich. "'Please Help Me': Kids With Guns Fueled a Record Number of School Shootings in 2021." *Washington Post*, December 31, 2021. www.washingtonpost.com/dc-md-va/2021/12/31/2021-school-shootings-record/.

Dawson, Ben. "The State of America's Children® 2021." *Children's Defense Fund*, April 13, 2021. www.myflfamilies.com/sites/default/files/2023-05/The-State-of-Americas-Children-2021.pdf.

Dorm, Emma, Bryan Hancock, Jimmy Sarakatsannis, and Ellen Viruleg. "COVID-19 and Education: The Lingering Effects of Unfinished Learning." *McKinsey & Company*, July 27, 2021. www.mckinsey.com/industries/education/our-insights/covid-19-and-education-the-lingering-effects-of-unfinished-learning.

Frog, Kermit the. *Before You Leap: A Frog's-eye View of Life's Greatest Lessons*. Des Moines: Meredith Books, 2006.

Gorman, Amanda. *The Hill We Climb: An Inaugural Poem*. New York: Random House, 2021.

Hooks, Bell. *All About Love: New Visions*. New York: HarperCollins, 2018.

Horowitz, Juliana Menasce, Kim Parker, Anna Brown, and Kiana Cox. "Amid National Reckoning, Americans Divided on Whether Increased Focus on Race Will Lead to Major Policy Change." *Pew Research Center's Social & Demographic Trends Project*, May 25, 2021. www.pewresearch.org/social-trends/2020/10/06/amid-national-reckoning-americans-divided-on-whether-increased-focus-on-race-will-lead-to-major-policy-change.

Jawando, Will. *My Seven Black Fathers*. New York: Farrar, Strause and Giroux, 2022.

McCarthy, Claire. "How Racism Harms Children." *Harvard Health Publishing*, January 8, 2020. www.health.harvard.edu/blog/how-racism-harms-children-2019091417788.

Martinez-Keel, Nuria. "Oklahoma Open Transfer Act Not Yet Making Transformational Waves." *The Oklahoman*, January 31, 2022.

National Association of Secondary School Principals. "Poverty and Its Impact on Students' Education." Last modified March 8, 2021. www.nassp.org/poverty-and-its-impact-on-students-education.

Nelson, Kadir. *Nelson Mandela*. New York: Katherine Tegen Books, 2019.

Putnam, Robert D. *Our Kids: The American Dream in Crisis*. New York: Simon & Schuster, 2016.

Rushnell, Squire D. *When God Winks at You*. Thomas Nelson, 2006.

Trent, Maria, Danielle G. Dooley, Jacqueline Dougé, Section on Adolescent Health, Council on Community Pediatrics,

Committee on Adolescence, Robert M. Cavanaugh Jr, et al. "Policy Statement: The Impact of Racism on Child and Adolescent Health." *American Academy of Pediatrics* 144, no. 2 (August 2019): e20191765. https://doi.org/10.1542/peds.2019-1765.

Washington, Denzel. *A Hand to Guide Me.* Des Moines: Meredith Books, 2006.

Winfrey, Oprah and Bruce D. Perry. *What Happened to You?: Conversations on Trauma, Resilience, and Healing.* London: Pan Macmillan, 2021.

ACKNOWLEDGMENTS

When I first met Laurel Thomas, *Write Your Heart Out*, at the Edmond Mitch Park YMCA in 2018, I was intrigued by her work as a ghostwriter and her upcoming novel. I was still working long hours at the Boys & Girls Club with no time or energy for writing, but conversations with Laurel planted a seed for meaningful work after I retired. When that day came, she became my first editor and coach. Gena Maselli, *Writing Momentum*, also provided helpful coaching support during the development of early drafts.

I am especially grateful for each of the Club members, staff, and volunteers who were willing to let me share their stories. I particularly want to thank AnaMarie, the former "Club kid" who not only was one of my first enthusiastic readers but also was responsible for much of the research regarding challenges facing the youth of our country.

Jennifer Fogg Lickteig, dear friend and former Boys & Girls Clubs of Oklahoma County board member, played a pivotal role during each step of the journey by reading various iterations always with enthusiasm and solid recommendations, and continuing to invest in creative ways to share the published book.

Another dear friend and accomplished writer Yvonne Maloan volunteered her developmental eye as well as much-needed emotional support on multiple occasions. Kathy Brown, Patsy Hosman, Donna Leftwich, Gil Mitchell, Mike Mize, Robin Schmidt, Casey Williams, and Zana Williams were terrific beta readers, providing affirming validation and encouragement.

The final version would have been very different, however, if my literary award-winning son John D. Sutter had not provided periodic encouragement as well as meaningful recommendations along the way. Thankfully, he relinquished that "three-questions-per-day" limit he had imposed as a teenager.

Bob Burke, renowned attorney, historian, and author of over 160 books, read both early and subsequent drafts and gave consistent assurances that these stories were important to share. He is also the person who pointed me toward FriesenPress. My FriesenPress publication specialist Julianne McCallum, promotion specialist Rebekah Caris, copy and proofreading editors, design experts, and other team members had the expertise and compassion to walk me through the publication process with confidence and grace, for which I am very thankful.

I shall remain forever grateful for David, my husband of forty-nine years, and for my son Ben, who consistently applauded my work at the Boys & Girls Club as well as the writing of this book—even when those efforts required long hours that resulted in limited family time.

Finally, I am deeply appreciative of you, my dear reader: not only because you have taken the time to read this labor of love, but because I trust that you will continue to make a positive difference for the kids in your community! Thank you!

ABOUT THE AUTHOR

JANE SUTTER is the former President & CEO of the Boys & Girls Clubs of Oklahoma County. She was Boys & Girls Clubs of America's Southwest Region Executive of the Year in 2017, was American Mothers, Inc. Oklahoma Mother of the Year in 2018, and named among Most Admired CEOs by the Journal Record in 2019. In retirement she volunteers extensively with the Harding Fine Arts Academy Foundation, Oklahoma City Public Schools Foundation's ReadOKC, Kirkpatrick Family Fund, and Westminster Presbyterian Church. Sutter holds a BS in Journalism and MS in Curriculum and Instruction from Oklahoma State University. She and her husband David live in Edmond, Oklahoma.

Printed in Canada